▼ The sandy beaches of Tel Aviv, on the Mediterranean Sea

Editorial Committee
RABBI WILLIAM CUTTER
ANNE LANSKI
RABBI MARK H. LEVINE
LESLEY LITMAN
ELLEN RANK
TAMMIE RAPPS
DEANNA SUSSMAN
VAVI TORAN
NINA WOLDIN

Design **BILL MILLER**
Cartographer **JIM MCMAHON**
Character illustration **GEO PARKIN**
Photo research **REBECCA BEHRMAN AND**
WILHELMINA ROEPKE
Project Manager **DENA NEUSNER**

SPECIAL THANKS to Allison Ofanansky for the
"Meet an Israeli" interviews on pages 47, 87, and 93,
and the "Meet a Palestinian" interview on page 69.

Copyright © 2011 Behrman House, Inc.
Published by Behrman House, Inc.
Springfield, NJ 07081
www.behrmanhouse.com
Visit www.behrmanhouse.com/EMI

ISBN 978-0-87441-800-2
Manufactured in the United States of America

Library of Congress Cataloging-in-Publication Data

Werner, Aviva.
 Experience modern Israel / by Aviva Werner.
   p. cm.
 Includes index.
 ISBN 978-0-87441-800-2
 1. Israel--Juvenile literature. 2. Israel--Description and
travel--Juvenile literature. I. Title.
  DS107.5.W47 2011
  956.9405'4--dc22
                         2010041876

"Ecology of Jerusalem" excerpt from *The Selected Poetry
of Yehuda Amichai*, trans. Chana Bloch and Stephen Mitchell
(Berkeley: University of California Press, 1996).

Please see photography credits on page 112.

NOTE TO READER:
In this book we use the terms BCE (Before
the Common Era) and CE (Common Era)
instead of BC and AD, which have Christian
origins.

▼ An ibex in the Ramon Crater,
in the Negev Desert

CONTENTS

I would like to express deepest thanks to the editorial committee members for their thoughtful and perceptive guidance in helping improve the manuscript for this book. I would also like to thank the staff at Behrman House—and particularly Dena Neusner, a professional editor in every sense of the word—for the opportunity to share my love of Israel with you. Finally, a special thank-you to my husband for all his support and encouragement. —A.W.

How to Use Modern Israel Online

http://www.behrmanhouse.com/EMI

Modern Israel Online is an interactive tour of Israel set in a Google Earth environment. You can explore dozens of preselected links to experience the sights and sounds of modern Israel.

Keywords found on the pages of *Experience Modern Israel* guide you on your virtual tour. You can even create your own tour of Israel, label your favorite places, and share them with your classmates.

▼ A patchwork of fields in the Galilee region

ONLINE SAFETY

Students: The Internet contains a wealth of interesting and fun resources, but remember to be safe when you're online. Get permission from an adult before exploring the Internet. Never give out personal information. Do not reply to e-mails from strangers. Do not log in or download anything without permission from an adult.

Educators and Parents: Behrman House regularly reviews and updates the links. However, content may change and links may lead to websites that are not monitored by Behrman House. Adult supervision is recommended when children are exploring Modern Israel Online.

1. Enter this website address...

http://www.behrmanhouse.com/EMI

2. Open Modern Israel Online...

First you'll need to click on **Google Earth** to download it to your computer. This is a free application that allows you to "fly" anywhere on Earth to view satellite imagery, maps, and other geographical content.

When Google Earth is downloaded, return to **www.behrmanhouse.com/EMI** and click on **Modern Israel Online**. View the instructions on the Welcome screen to get started.

3. Choose a keyword from the book...

Keywords indicate subjects that you can explore further in Modern Israel Online.

popular music

4. Start exploring!

"Fly" to any location.   Choose your topic here.   Click on the links.

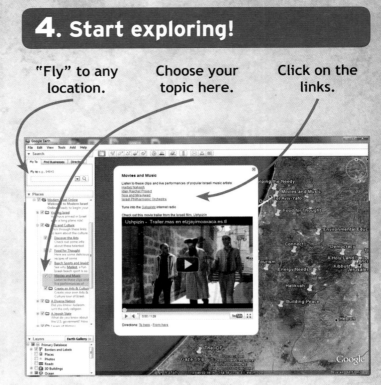

Use the keywords to find specific topics from the book, or browse the links for each chapter and subject. Watch video clips, listen to music, play games, and create your own tour.

For more detailed help and troubleshooting, open the "Modern Israel Online Help" document, which you can find on www.behrmanhouse.com/EMI and within the Modern Israel Online application itself.

ISRAEL IN PHOTOS
Did you know . . . ?

Mount Hermon

Golan Height

Haifa

Lake Kinneret

Mediterranean Sea

Tel Aviv-Jaffa

West Bank

Jerusalem

Dead Sea

Gaza

Be'er Sheva

NEGEV DESERT

Eilat

Gulf of Aqaba

N W E S

| 0 | | | | | 50 MI |
| 0 | | | | | 50 KM |

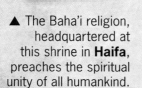

▲ The Baha'i religion, headquartered at this shrine in **Haifa**, preaches the spiritual unity of all humankind.

▶ The Azrieli Towers stand in the bustling city of **Tel Aviv**, which is the economic and cultural center of Israel.

▲ Visitors come to **Eilat** to swim, snorkel, sail, scuba dive, and watch dolphins play.

▲ A fisherman demonstrates old fishing techniques on **Lake Kinneret.**

▲ It snows every winter on **Mount Ḥermon**, the site of Israel's only ski resort.

▼ The Shrine of the Book in **Jerusalem** was designed to look like the clay jars in which the Dead Sea Scrolls were found.

◄ A drummer finds his rhythm at the Kotel, or Western Wall, in **Jerusalem**.

▶ Visitors are welcomed at this Bedouin hospitality tent in the Negev desert near **Be'er Sheva**.

▲ Plants grow and animals like this ibex roam at Ein Gedi, an oasis in the desert on the shores of the **Dead Sea.**

◄ Solomon's Pillars are a natural rock formation in Timna Valley National Park, in the **Negev Desert** north of Eilat.

1 INTRODUCTION
Visiting Israel

Sandals? Check. Bathing suit? Check. Passport, siddur, dictionary? Check, check, check. Umbrella? Is that something you should bring on a trip to Israel? Justin has no clue. It's his first time going to Israel, and he doesn't know what to expect.

Visiting Israel

He wonders if Israel is as rainy as his hometown of Seattle. He hopes there's something—anything—to do there for fun besides riding camels and dancing the hora. He worries about whether the local Israeli kids will understand him. He has no idea if there are even basketball courts in Israel. Justin can't imagine going two weeks without a game…or pizza. Do they eat pizza?

Jewish homeland

Of course, Justin does know a thing or two about Israel. He knows that it's the land God promised to our ancestors, according to the Bible; the land to which Moses led the Jewish people after the Exodus from Egypt; the land in which King Solomon built the Holy Temple and where Jews have lived for thousands of years.

Israel has always been the spiritual center of our people. For two thousand years, since being forced out of our homeland by the conquering Romans, Jews all over the world have prayed to return to Israel. And no matter where we are, we face in the direction of Jerusalem, and the **Kotel**, when we pray.

◀ A warm welcome at Ben-Gurion International Airport in Tel Aviv

virtual tour

▼ The city of **Jerusalem**

Modern state

Justin has also learned plenty about the modern State of Israel: how it was created in 1948 as a safe haven for the Jewish people. How it's the only country in the world where Jews are the majority, Jewish holidays are national holidays, and Hebrew is spoken on the streets. How this young nation is a leader in science and technology, and a popular tourist destination for its mix of archaeological sites, religious landmarks, and breathtaking scenery.

▲ **The Kotel (Western Wall)** is the holiest place in the world for Jews; we pray at the site where the **Temple** once stood.

Kotel

Nation in conflict

Then there are all the stories Justin reads in the headlines when he logs into his e-mail account. That Israel is a country in conflict with its neighbors; that terrorists have targeted Israelis; that the Palestinians want a state of their own; that peace with the Arabs is a dream, but quite far from a reality.

TIME TRAVEL

Almost any place you visit in Israel is bound to have biblical significance:

- The brave young shepherd boy David struck down the mighty Philistine warrior Goliath with his slingshot and stones in the **Elah Valley** (1 Samuel 17).

- The prophet Jonah ran away from God and boarded a ship at the port of Joppa, today called **Jaffa** (Jonah 1). After a great storm at sea, he spent three days in the belly of a great fish.

- The prophet Elijah challenged 450 prophets of the idol Baal to a contest on **Mount Carmel** (1 Kings 18), where he exposed them as frauds.

What is Israel really like?

All that history, politics, and Bible is important to know, but it doesn't tell Justin much about the *real* Israel…or help with the packing list. Justin is interested in what to expect when he gets off the plane.

In this book we'll answer Justin's questions and more. We'll meet Israeli teens and follow them to school, on a shopping trip, and to a soccer game. We'll visit some major cities and stop by an army induction ceremony. We'll learn about the diverse people who live in Israel and the achievements they have made in a short amount of time, in a tiny land, against great odds. We'll also explore some of the challenges Israel faces and see what the country is doing to address them.

▲ The **Azrieli Center**, Tel Aviv

So, on that note, we'll leave Justin to his packing. (FYI, Justin: The rainy season in Israel is from October to April, so that's the only time to bring an umbrella. In the summer the sun shines all day, every day.) We'll catch up with Justin again a little later to find out all about his trip.

What kinds of music do they listen to?

Are all Israelis either Jewish or Muslim?

Check off the things you think you'll find in Israel:

☐ Basketball ☐ Football ☐ Baseball ☐ Soccer

☐ Falafel ☐ Pizza ☐ Bagels ☐ Shawarma

☐ Hebrew ☐ English ☐ Arabic ☐ Russian

☐ Deserts ☐ Mountains ☐ Beaches ☐ Forests

Did you check them all? Go ahead and do it. Israel has a lot of variety for a tiny country the size of New Jersey.

◄ A **Bedouin** holds the Israeli flag during a ceremony in the desert near Eilat.

What are some of the great things Israel has to offer the world?

What kinds of schools do Israeli kids go to?

What do they do for fun?

say it in Hebrew

YOUR TURN: PACKING LIST

What would you bring on a visit to Israel? Think beyond the suitcase! In addition to sunglasses for the hot desert and hiking boots for the beautiful green fields of the Galilee, you'll need your eyes to see all there is to see, curiosity to try new foods, and much more.

My packing list:

2 ARTS AND CULTURE
Not Just Fun and Games

In a crowded alleyway in *Tzfat*, a microcalligrapher sits hunched over his work, painting colorful pictures composed of tiny Hebrew letters that will spell out verses from the Book of Genesis. Meanwhile in the ancient Roman amphitheater in Caesarea, fans fill the stadium seats, waiting to be captivated by the sound tapestry of their favorite Israeli hip-hop-rock-funk group. And in homes, apartments, and even tents throughout this tiny country, Israelis love to nosh on pita and hummus. Culture in Israel—from the fine arts to the patterns of everyday life—is alive and exciting.

National character

With Israelis hailing from so many different countries—from Russia, Poland, and Germany; from Yemen, Iraq, Ethiopia; from the United States and more—Israeli culture has lots of outside influences. As artists with different backgrounds have mingled in the galleries, concert halls, and streets of Tel Aviv and Jerusalem, an Israeli style has emerged, as unique and diverse as the Israeli people. Thus, landscape painting and photography often express individual views on living in the land. Music lyrics express the ups and downs of daily life, or traditional Jewish themes put to modern rhythms. Architecture combines traditional looks, such as white stone and rounded arches, with the needs of modern living. Israelis live in a place that is both new and very old at the same time, and Israeli culture reflects this.

microcalligraphy

◄ Home to the **Tel Aviv Performing Arts Center** (pictured here), the Israel Philharmonic Orchestra, and other world-class theaters, museums, opera, ballet, and nightclubs, Tel Aviv is the center of culture and entertainment in Israel.

Jewish influence

A primary influence on Israeli culture, of course, is Judaism, which is absolutely everywhere —on the street, in school, and on TV. Israelis build *sukkot* (huts) on Sukkot, have costume parades on Purim, close their shops on Shabbat, and eat in kosher restaurants.

▲ Both Jewish and Arab artists perform at the **Arab Hebrew Theatre of Jaffa**.

Arab influence

Arab influence is also an important part of Israeli culture, and you can see it clearly, for example, in street slang. Young trendsetters borrow much of their vocabulary from the Arabic language, including words like *aḥla* for "great," *sababa* for "it's all cool," and *yalla* for "now" or "let's go." There are acclaimed Arab-Israeli authors, Arab actors in Israeli movies, and Arab musicians and hip-hop groups. Israeli Jews and Arab Israelis play the same sports. However, for the most part, they listen to different music, produce different kinds of art, and read different books and newspapers.

▲ A **Purim parade** in Jerusalem

▼ **Roman amphitheater** in Caesarea

Off to school

To find out more about Israeli culture, let's peek in on a typical day for a typical teen. Tali, who lives in the city of Rishon Letzion, has invited us to tag along. Every school day—which in Israel means Sunday through Friday morning (yes, there's school on Sunday!)—she wakes up at 7:00 a.m. in order to make it to school by 8:15. In Israel, there are separate public school systems for **secular** Jews, religious Jews, and Arabs. Like Tali, the majority of Israeli students attend state schools, where they study subjects like science, history, literature, and art. Religious schools include more intensive Jewish studies, tradition, and observance. Students in Arab-Israeli schools study the same basic subjects as most Jewish Israelis, however subjects like literature and history focus more on the Arab experience.

Hebrew

One of the classes Tali takes in school today is Language and Literature, where she studies Hebrew grammar and writing. Hebrew is an ancient language that has been used in Jewish prayer and study for thousands of years. Then a man named Eliezer Ben-Yehuda came along at the turn of the twentieth century and led a movement to revive Hebrew as a language for everyday speech. He coined thousands of new words and phrases to adapt the language for twentieth-century living. For instance, there's no word in the Torah or Talmud for bicycle, so Ben-Yehuda created one: *ofanayim*.

Hebrew, once reserved for the synagogue and study hall, was now in the streets. It became the official language of the State of Israel and a common language among Jews of the world. Hebrew not only lets Tali buy an *agvaniyah* (tomato) in an Israeli **shuk** (market), but also connects Jews all over the world—including you—with each other and with Israel.

▲ The Hebrew word for **telephone** is… telephone. טֶלֶפוֹן

◄ Teen volunteers helping younger students on the first day of school

Literature

With the rebirth of the Hebrew language, many writers began creating Hebrew literature. Ḥayyim Naḥman Bialik, often called the greatest Hebrew poet of modern times, composed poetry in Hebrew that has since been put to music and translated into more than 30 languages. Today there is a fast-growing collection of Hebrew literature in every genre under the sun, from detective fiction to graphic novels to Holocaust literature. Thousands of new books are published in Hebrew each year, including original books by Israeli authors and books translated from other languages.

▲ **Eliezer Ben-Yehuda** insisted that his family speak only Hebrew at home. His son was the first child to grow up speaking modern Hebrew.

▲ Israelis at the annual **Hebrew Book Fair** in Jerusalem

▲ Israel's original literary trailblazers have passed on the pen to popular modern authors such as Arab Israeli **Sayed Kashua** (left) and **Etgar Keret** (right), both pictured here.

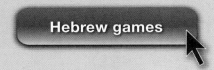

Hebrew games

POETRY AND METAPHOR

The air over Jerusalem is saturated with prayers and dreams

like the air over industrial cities.

It's hard to breathe.

And from time to time a new shipment of history arrives....

—from "Ecology of Jerusalem" by Yehuda Amichai

Circle the metaphors Yehuda Amichai uses to vividly describe how he experiences Jerusalem. Look at some photos of Jerusalem and make up your own metaphors to describe the ancient yet modern city, in the style of Amichai's poem.

Visual arts

Also on tap today in school is art class. The "Israeli" style of art is a mix of all the cultural influences found in Israel, as seen in everything from Yemenite-style jewelry to Eastern European silver Kiddush cups to traditional Ethiopian embroidery. Tali hopes to someday study at the Bezalel Academy of Arts and Design, named after Bezalel, who the Torah tells us was chosen by God to build the Tabernacle.

Some famous Israeli artists include Reuven Rubin, one of the first Israeli artists to achieve international recognition, Anna Ticho, whose drawings and paintings of the hills of Jerusalem are exhibited in major museums around the world, and Yaacov Agam, the famous sculptor and abstract artist, who enjoys international recognition, especially for his fountains in Tel Aviv and Paris.

◄ **"The Flutist"** by Reuven Rubin.

▲ **Kiddush cup**

artists

Themes in Israeli art

While biblical and **Zionist** (supporting the Jewish state) themes are common in Israeli art, they are by no means required. Israeli artists have been captivated by the surrounding landscape, creating works that depict olive and pomegranate trees, the sea, or grazing sheep. Some artists choose to express anti-war statements in their art, while others portray themes of national pride and allegiance.

ON THE STREET

Israelis aren't shy about their opinions. They plaster their politics on bus stops and spray-paint their views on bridge underpasses. The graffiti in cities around the country represents a wide variety of political and religious views.

There are even conversations via spray paint. One person paints *"Am Yisrael Chai"* (The Nation of Israel Lives), and another person adds some letters at the end to make *"Am Yisrael Chayav Li Kesef"* (The Nation of Israel Owes Me Money). The graffiti is illegal, but the law isn't enforced much.

▲ A popular **graffiti** phrase in Israel invokes the name of the Ḥasidic Rabbi Naḥman of Bratslav in a kind of chant. It reads, "Na Naḥ Naḥma Naḥman from Uman."

Poster art

Poster art is an important form of expression for Israeli artists, too. Israel has a tradition of producing Independence Day posters each year. The posters are a graphic commentary, offering a glimpse into Israel's national mood, concerns, achievements, and hopes for the future.

◀ This **1989 Independence Day poster** marks 41 years of Israel's independence and 40 years since the start of mass Jewish immigration to Israel. What symbols and themes do you see in this poster?

▲ A neighborhood of Tel Aviv known as **"The White City"** contains the largest group of buildings in the world built in the *Bauhaus style* of architecture. This style originated in Germany and was based on the use of simple, asymmetrical shapes.

Food favorites

School's out at 12:00 or 12:30, when Tali heads home for lunch or out to eat with friends. In Israel, lunch is the main meal of the day. Whereas fast food in America usually spells burgers or pizza (and you *will* find burger and pizza places in Israel), the most popular fast foods in Israel are **falafel** and *shawarma* (a pita sandwich made with turkey or lamb), which are Arab contributions to the national cuisine. Today Tali is in the mood for *bourekas* (puff pastries stuffed with various fillings) and Israeli salad, made of finely-chopped cucumbers and tomatoes.

▲ A **falafel** sandwich contains fried balls of ground chickpeas in a pita filled with sauces, salads, and pickles.

Recipes from around the world

Traditional Israeli cuisine goes way beyond falafel. As Jews from around the world have made *aliyah* (immigrated to Israel), they've brought along their traditional recipes from the Middle East, Europe, Africa, Asia, and North and South America. Eastern European Jews, for example, brought borscht (beet soup) to the Israeli table, while Jews from northern Africa contributed couscous.

▲ Baklava

Kosher quiz

A kosher lifestyle

Some foods that you won't find too easily in Israel—although they are available—are pork and shellfish. Under the Jewish dietary laws of *kashrut* (and also **Muslim** dietary laws), pig meat is off-limits. Judaism's kosher laws also require that milk and meat be kept separate and that kosher animals, like cows, be slaughtered in a specific way. The **Chief Rabbinate** supervises restaurants and issues kosher certificates to restaurants that follow all the laws of kashrut. Many secular Jews in Israel keep kosher—38 percent of them, according to a recent poll.

Jewish holidays have also shaped the eating habits of Israelis, with **sufganiyot** (jelly doughnuts) widely available on Ḥanukkah, an Israeli-style ḥaroset on Passover, and ḥallah available every Friday for Shabbat.

כשר M
מקדונלד'ס

▲ Many fast food chains—including **McDonald's**—maintain both kosher and non-kosher restaurants in Israel.

"A land of wheat, barley, grape, fig, and pomegranate; a land of olive trees and date honey..."
—Deuteronomy 8:8

▲ **Pomegranate**

Although the standard diet in Israel has diversified in the last few thousand years, these biblical species are still Israeli favorites. Pomegranates are especially significant in Jewish tradition. The plump red fruit is filled with hundreds of seeds—according to tradition, one pomegranate contains 613 seeds, to represent the 613 commandments in the Torah. Have you tasted each of these biblical species? If not, put them on the shopping list and share them with your family.

recipes

A **Middle Eastern feast**, meant to be shared ▶

Couscous, made of tiny pasta granules, is often steamed with spices, meat, or vegetables. ▼

Popular sports

After lunch today, Tali practices basketball with her youth league. Israelis love shooting hoops, kicking around a soccer ball, and following their favorite professional teams in the Hapoel and Maccabi leagues. Israel's soccer and basketball teams compete in Israel and Europe, and professional soccer players include both Jews and Arabs. Other popular sports in Israel include tennis, ice and roller hockey, and volleyball. Israel has won several Olympic medals, in sailing, canoeing, and judo. You'll find American sports like football and baseball in Israel, too, although the fans are mostly *olim* (immigrants to Israel) from countries where these sports are popular.

▲ **Hapoel** (in blue) vs **Ireland** in 2005 World Cup qualifier game.

"American football" ▶

Israelis (like much of the world) have different names for **soccer** and **football** than we do. ▶

▲ "football"

Fun and games at the beach

Many Israelis prefer to head to the beach for fun and games. Thanks to Lake Kinneret (also called the Sea of Galilee) in the north, the Mediterranean Sea to the west, and the Red Sea to the south there are plenty of opportunities for sailing, surfing, and swimming. *Matkot* is a popular beach sport in Israel. Imagine a game of tennis or paddleball, but without the net, the court, or the rules. The point is to hit the ball back and forth between players as long as possible without the ball touching the ground.

Children playing football in the four-thousand-year-old port city of **Akko** (or Acre). Known for its beautifully preserved walls, fortresses, and citadels, Akko has been home to the Canaanites, Greeks, Romans, Byzantines, Crusaders, Turks, and more. ▼

Jewish sports quiz

Maccabi games

The **Dead Sea** is the lowest place on Earth. With its high salt content and black mud full of nourishing minerals for the skin, it's also one of Israel's most popular tourist destinations. ▶

◀ **Beach sports** in Eilat, on the Red Sea.

Youth groups

In addition to sports, Israeli teens join a variety of youth groups, where they hike the country, sing around the campfire, attend summer camp, volunteer in their communities, and build friendships. More than 250,000 Israeli teens—representing the full range of the religious and political spectrums—participate in youth groups.

Tzofim, the Israel Scouts Federation, is Israel's national scouting club, with over 160 troops (a troop is called a *shevet*, or tribe) in six divisions—including Hebrew, Arab, Catholic, and **Druze**. The tribes meet regularly for service projects, nature trips, and cultural activities.

▼ **Tzofim**

MEET AN ISRAELI

When she was seven years old, Asala Shahada learned to swim in a cistern (a reservoir of water). Ten years later, Asala, an Arab-Israeli teen from the town of Sakhnin, won the gold medal for the 200-meter breaststroke at the 2005 **Maccabiah Games**. Often called the "Jewish Olympics," the Maccabiah Games are open to Jewish athletes from around the world and to all Israeli citizens, regardless of religion or ethnicity.

As 17-year-old Asala stood atop the championship podium, flanked by the silver and bronze medalists (both from the USA), she felt a surge of pride in her accomplishment. "The Maccabiah belongs not only to all the Jews," she said, "but also to all the Israelis, and I am a proud Israeli."

▲ A swimmer competes at the **Maccabiah Games**

The Olympic Games list their core values as friendship, excellence, and respect. List three additional core values for the Maccabiah Games:

1. _____

2. _____

3. _____

23

Popular music

On the way home, Tali listens to music on her phone, which is also an MP3 player. The music scene in Israel includes everything from religious to hip-hop, trance, and rap. Artists like Hadag Naḥash and Subliminal have created a unique Israeli hip-hop style. It's got the pounding rhythms of American hip-hop, but the words—in Hebrew, of course—make all the difference. While American hip-hop artists sing a lot about partying and violence, Israeli hip-hop addresses issues of politics, economics, and the Arab-Israeli conflict. One of Hadag Naḥash's biggest hits is "The Sticker Song," whose lyrics are slogans found on Israeli bumper stickers, such as "a strong nation makes peace" and "long live the King Messiah." A hit song by Israeli rapper Mook E features the chorus, "everyone talks about peace, no one talks about justice."

▼ Israelis love to dance. **The Karmiel Dance Festival** draws 5,000 dancers and more than 250,000 spectators each year.

Many Israeli singers and musicians have made it big on the international scene. Noa (Achinoam Nini) is a leading international concert and recording artist who has performed in New York, throughout Europe, and even in Italy for the Pope. The Idan Raichel Project, a collaboration of musicians from different Israeli cultural backgrounds, has sold triple platinum and performed around the world. Yael Naim's song "New Soul" made the Billboard Top 10, and Miri Ben-Ari has performed her hip-hop violin music with the likes of Kanye West, Jay-Z, and Wyclef Jean.

▲ Hip-hop artist **Subliminal**

popular music

Palestinian music

Palestinian music—the music of much of Israel's Arab population—reflects struggle with Israel and love of the land of **Palestine**. The rap group DAM was the first Palestinian hip-hop group when it was founded in the late 1990s. The group's lyrics often express frustration at feeling like second-class citizens in Israel.

Musical dialogue

At the 2009 Eurovision Song Contest, Noa performed the song "There Must Be Another Way" together with Mira Awad, a popular Arab-Israeli singer and actress. The song's English, Hebrew, and Arabic lyrics call for hope, understanding, and respect for the humanity of others. Although they didn't win the contest, Noa and Awad's cooperation demonstrated a commitment to dialogue between Israeli Jews and Arabs.

▲ Noa (left) and Mira Awad (right) perform at the **Eurovision** Song Contest.

▼ Arab dancers perform the **dabke**.

Israel Philharmonic

Classical and folk music

Israel has produced some first-rate classical composers and musicians, including world-famous violinist Itzhak Perlman. The Israel Philharmonic Orchestra is Israel's leading symphony orchestra. And, not surprisingly, Israel is the hub of Orthodox Jewish music, in which the words are typically taken from religious texts and the melodies are often a mix of rock and **klezmer** (Jewish folk music). Traditional Palestinian folk music is played at Arab-Israeli weddings and other ceremonies, accompanied by the *dabke*, a popular line dance.

Television

After basketball practice and a quick shower, Tali unwinds by watching TV. In addition to original Israeli TV programs, many Israelis have cable or satellite systems that offer international movies and shows, often with subtitles. Tali's favorites are reality TV shows, and she has had plenty to choose from over the years. For example, there is *Kochav Nolad* (*A Star Is Born*), Israel's version of *American Idol* and a career-launcher for many Israeli pop singers, and *Ha'aḥ Hagadol* (*Big Brother*), whose finale sent ratings through the roof. Some Israeli TV shows have been picked up and adapted for American TV as well, including HBO's *In Treatment* and NBC's *Phenomenon*.

▲ A scene from the movie **Ushpizin**

Radio

Tali makes sure her homework is all done before turning in for the night. She sets her alarm to wake up to Galgalatz, one of two official Army radio stations in Israel. Station broadcasters—who are also soldiers—broadcast mainly music and traffic reports. The station plays an interesting mix of music styles and you can never predict what's coming next —everything from American musician Bob Dylan to Spanish singer Julio Iglesias to Israeli Idan Raichel. Israeli teens love Galgalatz. You can also listen to the station online from anywhere in the world. The other official Army radio station is called Galei Tzahal (or Israel Defense Forces Waves) which broadcasts more news and traffic reports than music.

Internet radio

▼ More than 150 films are screened over the course of the ten-day **Jerusalem Film Festival**.

◄ **Kol Yisrael** radio studio

Film

There's plenty to choose from in the movie theater, so grab some popcorn. Israeli films have been nominated for Academy Awards in the United States for best foreign-language film, and are represented in film festivals and contests throughout the world. The movies commonly address themes of war, aliyah, differences between Jews and Arabs, and similar subjects that speak to the Israeli experience. In *Waltz with Bashir*, a 2008 animated film, for example, an Israel Defense Forces (IDF) soldier searches for lost memories of the 1982 Lebanon War. *Ushpizin*, a 2004 Israeli film, explores the daily lives of ultra-Orthodox Jews whose faith is tested during the holiday of Sukkot.

◄ A **Shrek the Third** movie poster. American movies are popular in Israel.

movie trailer

YOUR TURN: TRY SOMETHING NEW

What are your favorite foods, music, TV shows, sports?

School subject: _____

Food: _____

Music: _____

TV show or movie: _____

Sport: _____

In what ways are your tastes similar to or different from Tali's?

Circle the names of all the Israeli writers, artists, musicians, TV shows, and movies in this chapter that you have read, seen, or heard. Now look at some Israeli art online, listen to some Israeli music, and read some Israeli poems or books until you have circled a dozen or more names on these pages.

3 A DIVERSE NATION
Israeli Salad

The modern State of Israel is a vibrant mix of different religions and cultures. Israelis include Jews, Muslims, and Christians; secular and religious; native-born sabras, Arabs, and immigrants from all over the world. In some towns and cities, these various groups of Israelis live together side-by-side, and in other areas they live separately in their own communities.

Jewish diversity

Take Tzfat (also called Safed), for example. It's a Jewish city with almost 100 percent Jewish citizens. Just as Jews are the majority in Tzfat, Jews make up the vast majority of Israel's diverse population—75.4% of all Israelis are Jewish. Yet even amongst Israeli Jews there is exceptional diversity.

There's a whole spectrum of religious observance among Jews, from secular to religious Zionists, ḥaredi (ultra-Orthodox), and Ḥasidic. There's a rainbow of skin color, from light-skinned Russian Jews to darker Ethiopian Israelis. There are **Sephardic** Jews (with Spanish or Portuguese lineage), **Mizraḥi** (Middle Eastern) Jews, and **Ashkenazic** Jews (with European lineage), each with their own liturgy (prayer service), history, and culture. There are also sabras, native-born Israelis, many of whose

▲ An **Ethiopian Jewish** bead-maker

parents, grandparents, or great-grandparents founded the State with their sweat and dedication. From twelve tribes in biblical times, we've blossomed into many more varied groups.

◀ Jews born in Israel are called **sabras**. The term also refers to the fruit of a cactus, which is prickly on the outside but sweet on the inside.

▲ An **Orthodox Jewish** boy

▲ A **Druze** woman and child

Other ethnic groups

Although Israel is a Jewish state, there are many other ethnic groups that call Israel home. Arab citizens include Muslims, Christians, **Bedouins**, and Druze, each with their own traditions, lifestyles, and communities. In addition, foreign workers come to Israel from Thailand, Romania, West Africa, and the Philippines.

▼ **Diversity** in the Israel Defense Forces

A city known best as the sixteenth-century birthplace of Kabbalah (Jewish mysticism), **Tzfat** is also a modern artist colony. ▼

ISRAELI SALAD

Israel is a country rich with many cultures. Each of its immigrant groups arrived on Israeli soil with its own customs, history, and language. Israeli diversity could be compared to a salad bowl. Like a salad, each ingredient (each ethnic group) retains its own distinct flavor, yet each adds to the rich flavor of the dish (the State of Israel).

With a partner, explain these other metaphors that have been used to describe Israel's diversity. Israel is:

- like a melting pot, because _____
- like a mosaic, because _____
- like a stew, because _____

Which metaphor do you like best? Why?

Immigrant Backgrounds

Let's meet Yehudit, who goes to a public school for secular Jewish students in Be'er Sheva. Yehudit's school friends come from a wide variety of Jewish backgrounds. In today's history class, Yehudit and her classmates will present projects about the various *aliyot* (immigrations to Israel) that have brought Jews from around the world to Israel. Yehudit is proud of her Ethiopian heritage, but she is nervous about highlighting her differences.

Yemenite Jews

First Yehudit's friend Shlomo presents his report. Let's listen: "After the United Nations declared a Jewish state in the Land of Israel, Muslims in Yemen started rioting and destroying Jewish homes and businesses," explains Shlomo. "It wasn't safe for Jews in Yemen anymore, so between 1949 and 1950 Israel brought 49,000 Yemenite Jews home to Israel in what was called Operation Magic Carpet.

Yemenite women

"My grandparents had never seen an airplane before and were afraid to board, but their rabbi reminded them that God promised to bring the Jewish people to our land on 'wings of eagles.'

"We Yemenite Jews have our own unique Hebrew pronunciation. We have our own synagogues where we keep the traditions of our ancestors, including the henna ceremony. My sister had this before her wedding. She was dressed in an embroidered costume with an elaborate headpiece and jewelry, and painted with henna makeup."

A Yemenite bride

Yemenite wedding

Operation Magic Carpet

Russian Jews

Now it's Boris's turn. "My family came from Russia in the former Soviet Union," he begins. "This was in the 1980s, when there was a lot of anti-Semitism there. Many Jews applied for exit visas, which gave them official permission to leave, but most of them were turned down. They were called **refuseniks** and were considered traitors just for requesting a visa. Jews around the world protested, 'Let My People Go!'

"Eventually the Soviet Union started granting exit visas. When it collapsed in 1991, even more Soviet Jews made aliyah—over one million people came to Israel. A lot of the Jewish *olim* (immigrants to Israel) brought along non-Jewish husbands, wives, and relatives. This decreased the Jewish majority in Israel and led to questions about marriage, conversion, and army service for non-Jewish Israeli citizens.

Soviet immigrant girl

refuseniks

"As Russian Jews brought their culture to Israel, many established orchestras and theaters here. I'm grateful that my family made aliyah from the Soviet Union," Boris adds. "I hear it's awfully cold in Russia."

31

Ethiopian Jews

Now it's Yehudit's turn. "My report is about the Jews who came to Israel from Ethiopia," she begins. "My family is **Beta Israel**, from a tribe descended from King Solomon. In 1984, about 8,000 Jewish Ethiopians undertook a long, dangerous walk to Sudan to airplanes that would smuggle them to Israel in what was called Operation Moses.

Operation Solomon

"When we got here, many Israelis questioned whether we were really one of the ten Lost Tribes of Israel. The Chief Rabbinate made all the new immigrants convert to Judaism, even though we had worked hard for centuries to stay Jewish. My parents were insulted.

"Another 14,000 Ethiopian Jews came to Israel in 1991, in the top-secret Operation Solomon. A lot of Ethiopian Israeli olim have had a hard time adjusting to high-tech Western life in Israel. Many are still very poor, illiterate in both Hebrew and Amharic (one of the languages of Ethiopia), or unemployed. Many of their children struggle with poverty, racism, and inadequate schooling. I am lucky that our school has social workers to help Ethiopian Israelis like me and my family with extra enrichment and catch-up classes.

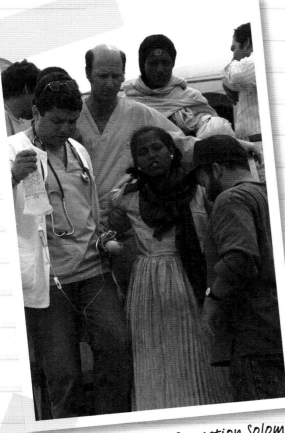
Operation Solomon

"We Beta Israel observe **Sigd**, a holiday that celebrates the acceptance of the Torah. I'm proud that in 2008, Sigd was declared an Israeli national holiday." Yehudit takes a deep breath, relieved to be done.

Sigd

Ethiopian Jews celebrate Sigd.

Anglo Jews

Next up is Ilana, the new girl in school. "I'm doing my report on Anglo Jews—Jews who have come to Israel from English-speaking countries like Canada, the United States, Australia, and South Africa.

"More than 100,000 immigrants have made aliyah from North America since Israel was founded in 1948. Mostly they come for Zionist reasons—they love Israel, the Jewish state. My family made aliyah a few months ago from Toronto, Canada. We're still learning the language, and sometimes my brother refuses to go to school because he doesn't understand the other kids, but things are getting better.

Natan Sharansky (middle), Chairman of the Jewish Agency for Israel, greets new Olim on their arrival in Israel.

American Jews making aliyah

"I love how the Jewish holidays are everywhere in Israel. In Toronto, we had a fun Purim parade in the synagogue every year, but here in Be'er Sheva, there's an enormous Purim parade with thousands of people and costumes and performances and floats and events all over the city. It's an adjustment being in a new country, but it's great." Ilana takes her seat, and Yehudit smiles. She's thankful to be just like everyone else in her class—unique and Israeli.

A holy land

Although Israel is a Jewish state, there are many ethnic groups and religions that call Israel home, and many sites in Israel—especially in Jerusalem, Israel's

▲ The **Dome of the Rock** in Jerusalem is the third holiest site in Islam. It sits on the Temple Mount, overlooking the Kotel.

capital city—are important to Christians and Muslims as well as Jews. In fact, the Old City of Jerusalem is divided into four quarters—Muslim, Christian, Armenian, and Jewish.

Jews come from around the world to pray at the Kotel. Christians view Jerusalem as holy for its significance in the life and death of Jesus, while Muslims revere it as the place of Muhammad's ascension to heaven. All told, Jerusalem houses more than 1,000 synagogues, more than 150 churches, and some 70 mosques.

Muslim and Christian Arabs

The city of Nazareth, the childhood home of Jesus and a holy place for Christians around the world, is actually one of the largest Arab cities in Israel. Arab citizens—those who speak Arabic and who identify with the Arab people, regardless of their religion—make up 20 percent of the population of Israel. The majority of these Arab citizens of Israel (about 70 percent) are Muslim, while 9 percent of Israel's Arab population is Christian, and the rest are Bedouins and Druze.

Many Arabs—both Muslim and Christian—consider themselves Palestinian and have family members who live in the **West Bank**, **Gaza Strip**, and neighboring Arab countries.

▲ The **Church of the Holy Sepulchre** stands on the site where the Christian New Testament says Jesus died and was buried and resurrected.

▼ The **Baha'i Shrine and Gardens** in Haifa is the international headquarters of the **Baha'i** faith.

holy sites

▲ **Bedouins** are a nomadic or semi-nomadic Arabic people who live primarily in deserts, in villages that aren't found on a map and don't have basic services like running water or electricity. In Israel, they live mostly in the Negev and the Galilee regions. In the 1960s, the Israeli government built towns for the Bedouins and encouraged them to settle as permanent residents. However, much of Israel's Bedouin population is still nomadic.

▲ An Arab man sells spices at the **shuk**, or market.

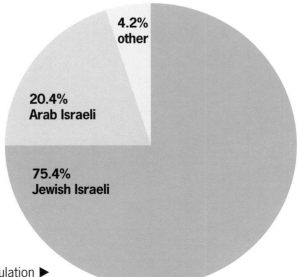

▲ The **Druze** speak Arabic and keep their religious practices secret from outsiders. There are about 120,000 Druze living in Israel.

Israel's population ▶

4.2% other

20.4% Arab Israeli

75.4% Jewish Israeli

Getting along

For the most part, Israel's diverse peoples get along. They walk the same streets, shop in the same stores, and attend the same universities. However, tensions between groups sometimes boil over, especially over religion. For instance, friction between religious and secular Jews led to riots in 2009 when the city of Jerusalem decided to open a public parking lot on Shabbat. And tension between Jews and Arabs has led to stone throwing and other violence. Each community in Israel has differing needs and also differing opinions on how, for example, government money should be distributed.

▲**Orthodox** Jewish boys

YOU'VE NEVER SEEN ANYTHING LIKE IT

Diversity in Israel isn't just about religion. It's about people who are different in many other ways as well—including people with disabilities.

Visitors to the Dialogue in the Dark exhibit at the Israel Children's Museum in Holon, just south of Tel Aviv, enter a world of darkness to experience two hours of blindness. Blind guides lead visitors through seven familiar environments—including a store, a busy intersection, and a park—that are transformed into unfamiliar settings when the lights are out.

Sighted visitors learn to appreciate the strengths of the blind and experience their own limits. The blind guides, too, are empowered as their disability is turned into a strength. They are now the experts, helping their visitors navigate pitch blackness.

Create your own world of darkness. Take turns guiding blindfolded friends through a maze of desks, chairs, and hallways. Afterward discuss your difficulties and any other perceptions. Were you scared? Were your other senses heightened?

▼ **Israel Children's Museum** in Holon

Dialogue in the Dark

מוזיאון הילדים הישראלי · חולון

Separate worlds

Separation (official or not) of different communities by neighborhoods, schools, or army units is not helpful in easing conflict, preventing stereotypes, or integrating minority groups into the larger Israeli society. Orthodox Jews, for example, tend to live in neighborhoods separate from secular Jews, in part because they do not drive on Shabbat, and so all members of a community live near their synagogue. They send their children to religious schools only, and if they serve in the army, they generally serve in religious units. Many Russian immigrants to Israel separate themselves by clinging to the Russian language. And since Arab citizens have their own religion, culture, and language, they tend to live in their own neighborhoods and send their kids to Arab schools and youth groups. They also don't serve in the army, with some exceptions.

▲ Arab demonstrators

SPOTLIGHT ON IDAN RAICHEL PROJECT

▲ Idan Raichel

It's not just a band; it's a multicultural phenomenon. With its blend of Ethiopian, Caribbean, Arabic, and Hebrew music, the Idan Raichel Project took the Israeli music scene by storm in 2002.

The music is a fusion of the different musical sounds, instruments, and languages you might hear in the clubs and on the streets of Tel Aviv. Idan Raichel writes and arranges the songs, and singers and musicians of various ethnic backgrounds perform them.

Cabra Casay, one of Idan's performers, was born in a refugee camp in Sudan while her family was journeying from Ethiopia to Israel.

Singer and actress **Mira Awad** was born to a Palestinian father and a Bulgarian mother in an Arab village in northern Israel.

Ravid Kahalani combines African and Arabic influences with his own Yemenite Jewish musical roots.

Listen to music by the Idan Raichel Project and choose a song you like. With a partner, write the lyrics for a song about peace and understanding, and set your words to the rhythm and beat of the song you chose.

4 A JEWISH STATE
There's No Place Like Home

On a typical Friday afternoon in cities across the State of Israel, businesses close up earlier than usual. Shopkeepers pack up and put away their merchandise, wishing their last customers of the day a warm "Shabbat shalom." For Israelis, Jewish culture is everywhere—not just in the synagogue, but on the street, in school, and on TV. The typical work week and school week is Sunday through Friday morning, with Shabbat the official day off, and Jewish holidays are national holidays.

Religion and Government

Unlike the separation of church and state in the United States, there's no official separation of religion and government in Israel. On the contrary, by law the army and all government facilities serve kosher food, there's a minister of religious affairs, and official laws limit raising pigs (non-kosher animals) and prohibit publicly displaying ḥameitz (leavened bread) on Passover. In addition, the government financially supports religious institutions, including schools, *yeshivot* (institutions for advanced Jewish learning), and synagogues. Israel is a Jewish country—no doubt about it.

▲ The Israeli flag was designed to resemble a **tallit**—a prayer shawl—with a Magen David (Jewish star) in the center.

women

▲ Jews come from all over the world to celebrate becoming a **bar or bat mitzvah** in the Land of Israel.

SOMETHING TO SING ABOUT

On **Yom Ha'atzma'ut** (Israel Independence Day) in 2008, Israel set the Guinness World Record for the most people singing a national anthem simultaneously. Jewish groups around the world joined together to sing **"Hatikvah"** as a sign of unity, hope, and love of Israel.

"Hatikvah" is about the eternal longing of the Jewish people for the land of Israel during millennia of living in foreign lands. Today, with a free and independent State of Israel, the dream is finally realized. That sure is something to sing about.

Rewrite "Hatikvah" in your own words. What does it mean? _____

_____

_____

_____

Does "Hatikvah" speak to all Israelis? What about Sephardic Jews? Where they come from, Zion wasn't necessarily "toward the East." What about Arab Israelis, who aren't Jewish?

HATIKVAH הַתִּקְוָה

As long as deep in the heart,

The soul of a Jew yearns,

And toward the East,

An eye looks to Zion,

Our hope is not yet lost,

The hope of two thousand years,

To be a free people in our land,

The land of Zion and Jerusalem.

—composed in 1878 by Naphtali Herz Imber

Hatikvah

▼ Teens celebrate **Yom Yerushalayim**, Jerusalem Day

A democracy

Israel is a democracy, as well as a Jewish state. This means that all of Israel's citizens—Jewish or not—enjoy basic rights regardless of the God they worship (or don't), the color of their skin, their gender, or the customs they practice. They have freedom of religion and speech, and can vote and be elected. An Arab can—and does—sit on the Israeli Supreme Court, a woman can—and did—serve as prime minister, and there are Druze and other minorities in the **Knesset** (the Israeli Parliament). And unlike many of its neighbors, Israel protects freedom of speech and the press.

▲ **Golda Meir** was Israel's prime minister from 1969 to 1974, and only the third female prime minister in the world.

▶ **Benjamin Netanyahu**, elected in 1996 and again in 2009, is the first prime minister to have been born in the modern State of Israel.

Israeli government 101

When you keep hearing about this party and that party in Israel, it seems like the country is one big blowout bash. But seriously, we're talking political parties. Israel's government is a **parliamentary democracy**, which means it's based on a multiparty system. Political parties represent many different social groups. The biggest parties are Kadima, Likud, and Labor. In addition, there's the Shas party, which caters to mostly ḥaredi (ultra-Orthodox) Sephardic Jews; Ra'am-Ta'al, which represents Arab Israelis; a party called Meretz that is backed by environmentally-conscious political progressives; and many more.

▲ This tall **menorah** stands outside the Knesset building.

Knesset

▼ The **Knesset building**, in Jerusalem

The Knesset

The Knesset is the legislative branch of the Israeli government, much like the U.S. Congress and the Parliament of Canada. When elections are held, voters choose a political party, rather than individual representatives. The more votes a party receives, the more members of that party are seated as members of the Knesset. The party with the most votes gets the most Knesset seats and chooses the prime minister. This system is very different from the United States, where voters essentially cast their ballots for the candidate rather than the party.

► Prime Minister **Menaḥem Begin** signed the first peace treaty between Israel and an Arab state (Egypt), in 1979. He is pictured here presenting the treaty to the Knesset.

Building a coalition

The winning party often does not have a majority (61 out of a total of 120 seats) and therefore has to cooperate with other parties to form what's called a coalition government. This system can give disproportionate influence to small political parties, which might join with the winning party in exchange for support on issues that are important to them.

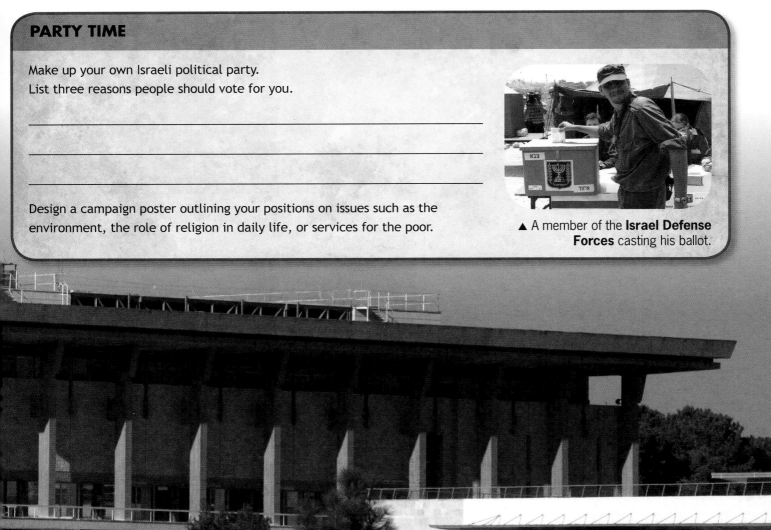

PARTY TIME

Make up your own Israeli political party.
List three reasons people should vote for you.

_____

_____

_____

Design a campaign poster outlining your positions on issues such as the environment, the role of religion in daily life, or services for the poor.

▲ A member of the **Israel Defense Forces** casting his ballot.

The Law of Return

Let's join Eden, a sports fan from Akko, as he cheers on his hometown soccer team, Hapoel Akko. One of Eden's favorite players made *aliyah* from Argentina under the **Law of Return**, which offers all Jews the right to Israeli citizenship. Israel is a home not only for the people who live in Israel, but also for the entire Jewish people wherever they may be.

The Law of Return guarantees a refuge where Jews can go to be in charge of themselves, in a Jewish state, free from fear of anti-Semitism. This principle has led to waves of immigration, as Jews have fled persecution and hardship in Yemen, Ethiopia, Russia, and other countries.

Some say the Law of Return discriminates against non-Jews, who have a much harder time becoming Israeli citizens. Others counter that, as a Jewish state, Israel has the right and the obligation to welcome Jews from around the world.

▲ Proudly waving the **Israeli flag**

Law of Return

▼ View of **Jerusalem** as seen from the ancient, and ethnically diverse, Old City

Who is a Jew?

In a Jewish state, the question of how to define someone as a Jew is both personal and political. The Law of Return includes anyone whose parent or grandparent was Jewish, as well as anyone who has converted to Judaism (including Conservative or Reform conversions outside of Israel). In 1970, the law was expanded to welcome spouses of Jews as well.

However, this definition of "who is a Jew" is broader than the Orthodox interpretation of *halachah* (Jewish religious law), which says a person must be born to a Jewish mother or convert according to strict Orthodox standards in order to be considered a Jew.

Since the Israeli Chief Rabbinate abides by Orthodox *halachah* on personal issues like marriage, divorce, and funerals, this creates a problem for thousands of Israelis who became citizens under the Law of Return but are not considered Jewish by the Chief Rabbinate. This group also includes Americans who have converted to Judaism within the Conservative or Reform movements, and therefore are considered Jewish by the State but not by the rabbinate.

Liberal Judaism

Most Jews in Israel are either Orthodox or **secular**, and Reform and Conservative Judaism, which thrive in America and Canada, have a far smaller presence there. Orthodox and ultra-Orthodox Jews live according to a strict interpretation of halacha, Jewish religious law from the Torah, Talmud, and other sources. Secular Jews, on the other hand, identify with a cultural Judaism. Although they do not affiliate with a particular movement or synagogue, many do observe Jewish holidays and Shabbat and even keep kosher. There's a powerful and fast-growing phenomenon of secular Jews engaging in religious text study and observance in an emergent form of Judaism that is uniquely Israeli.

The Reform movement, called **Progressive Judaism**, and the Conservative one, called the **Masorti Movement**, are small in Israel, where the old joke says "the synagogue I don't belong to is Orthodox." But these movements are growing, with more Israelis each year identifying with them as acceptable alternatives to Orthodox affiliation.

▲ **Masorti Youth** participate in a variety of religious, cultural, and social action programs. This child is waving a lulav and etrog in celebration of Sukkot.

Orthodox and secular conflicts

There are a number of hot political issues dividing Israelis, and Israel often has to perform a delicate balancing act between groups that disagree on the role of religion in everyday life.

For instance, only Orthodox conversions to Judaism are accepted under Israeli religious law, a Jew and a non-Jew may not marry each other, and civil marriage (marriage without rabbis involved) doesn't exist. Many couples who are unable or unwilling to abide by Orthodox rules instead go overseas to get married, most often to nearby Cyprus. Some people see the state's strict adherence to Jewish law as a violation of citizens' democratic rights. Christians, Arabs, and Druze have their own religious authorities that regulate these issues in their communities.

Army service

Another divisive political issue is army duty. Eden knows that he'll be required to join the Israel Defense Forces at age 18, as are most men and women. But there are some major exceptions. Orthodox Jews are exempt from serving in the IDF while they are studying in a **yeshiva**. Many ultra-Orthodox men devote their whole lives to yeshiva study and will never serve because of this exemption. Secular Israelis say that this isn't fair; while secular Israelis risk their lives defending their country, they see Orthodox Jews bent over ancient books in air-conditioned study halls.

◀ An Israeli soldier wearing **tefillin**, ritual prayer items

national service

▼ Thousands of **ḥaredim** demonstrating for street closings on Shabbat

Many Orthodox men do fulfill their obligation to army service, and Orthodox women often do a year of national service instead. However, most ultra-Orthodox Jews do not serve. They argue that Torah study preserves a sacred heritage that has kept us together as a nation through thousands of years of **Diaspora** (scattering around the world) and assimilation (absorbing characteristics of other nations).

Other army exemptions are given to Arab Israelis because of potentially divided loyalties, since most of Israel's military conflicts are with Arab states or Palestinians. Some Arab Israelis, notably the Druze, do serve in the army, however.

▶ According to ultra-Orthodox Jews, while the army preserves the physical survival of the country, **Torah learning** ensures the spiritual survival of the Jewish people.

DEBATE IT

Buses are the most common way that Israelis get around town—except on Shabbat, that is. In the Jewish state, most buses do not run on Shabbat or Jewish holidays. Religious Jews support the ban on buses running on Shabbat, a day of rest, arguing that it enriches Israel's Jewish character and enhances the sanctity of the day. Secular Israelis, on the other hand, argue that the ban intrudes on their personal freedom and discriminates against those who can't afford to buy a car. Should public buses be banned from running on Shabbat in Israel? Have a debate.

NO BUSES ON SHABBAT vs LIFT THE BAN

What other solution can you think of?

Minority groups

The majority of Israel's citizens are Jewish. But nearly a quarter of Israel's 7.5 million people are not. There are plenty of minority groups living in Israel, including Muslims, Christians, Bedouins, and Druze, and Israel protects their freedom to practice these religions, even while establishing Judaism as the state religion.

▲ **Muslim man** at prayer.

▶ Most street and highway signs in Israel are **trilingual**— in Hebrew, Arabic, and English.

Two official languages

"Watch out for the sweeper," screams Eden in Hebrew at Hapoel Akko's center forward. Hebrew and Arabic— Eden's two best languages—are the official languages of Israel. As a Jewish state, modern Israel has revived the language of ancient Israel and the Torah, albeit with a modern vocabulary to accommodate modern concepts.

Jewish Israeli kids like Eden speak Hebrew in school, learn basic Arabic as a core class, and study English as an elective. Arab-Israeli students, on the other hand, speak Arabic in school and learn Hebrew and English. By law, Arab citizens have the right to receive information they can understand, and so public TV shows, medicine labels, election information, and other important things to know are translated into Arabic.

National holidays

As the blue-and-white-uniformed players continue the race toward the goal, Eden is reminded of the blue and white Israeli flag. The flag flies high at all official ceremonies, including those on Yom Ha'atzma'ut, Israel Independence Day, which is celebrated throughout Israel with ceremonies, barbecues, and singing and dancing in the street.

Like Presidents' Day, Thanksgiving, and Christmas in the United States, Jewish holidays are national holidays in Israel. Because Israel supports freedom of religion, however, schools and businesses have several optional holiday calendars from which to choose. Thus an Arab school does not have to celebrate Sukkot but will typically close on Muslim holidays, such as Eid al Fitr, which marks the end of fasting during the month of Ramadan.

▲ The blessing of the **Kohanim** (priests) at the Kotel on Sukkot

MEET AN ISRAELI

Sixteen-year-old Ortal grew up in a "somewhat traditional but not really religious" family in Yishuv Eli, where she attended a religious public school and gradually became more religious. "I understand both the secular and the religious worlds," she says, "so I know that the differences between them are not so great."

To help raise awareness, Ortal hosted a teen radio show on which she interviewed religious and secular students who met through a group called *Gesher* (Bridge). "They became good friends, which surprised them," she said.

Ortal says she'd like to do national service organizing and leading such groups. Ortal thinks it's important to bring together young people from the "extremes of Israeli society—the very secular and the *ḥaredi*. Some of them have hardly even talked to someone from outside their community."

"Israel is multi-cultural," Ortal says. "We're all part of the nation of Israel. We can take a step in the right direction and be friends."

▶ **Israel Independence Day** fireworks

5 LAYERS OF HISTORY
War and Peace

Let's follow Dalia, a student from Tel Aviv, on a field trip through three thousand years of Israel's history. Dalia is interested in both ancient and modern history… and in a land like Israel, with streets named after rabbinic sages and buildings made of the same Jerusalem stone that has been used since the time of King David, there are plenty of opportunities for exploring both past and present.

"If I forget you, O Jerusalem, let my right hand wither, let my tongue stick to my palate if I cease to think of you, if I do not keep Jerusalem in memory even at my happiest hour."

—Psalms 137:5-6

Jerusalem

Ancient History

Dalia's class gathers in the archaeology wing of the Israel Museum in Jerusalem, where they are surrounded by ancient pottery and other artifacts. The Land of Israel has a very long history for the Jewish people. According to the Bible, Moses led our ancestors to the Land of Israel (then called Canaan) following the miraculous Exodus from slavery in Egypt and the forty years of wandering in the desert. Later, King Solomon built the **First Temple** in Jerusalem, and it served as the center of Jewish life and worship for hundreds of years.

▼ The **Kotel** was a supporting outer wall of the Second Temple. Jews come from all over the world to pray here, at our holiest site. Visitors often insert small slips of paper with their prayers between the stones of the Wall.

Many civilizations

The Land of Israel lies at the crossroads of important trade routes between Africa and Asia and has been subjected to one invading army after another, including the Assyrians, Babylonians, and Persians. The Temple was destroyed, and a **Second Temple** was built. Over the centuries, the Land of Israel became home to many more civilizations, including the Greeks and the Romans. Jesus, whom Christians came to worship as the son of God, was born in Judea (now Israel) when it was under Roman rule, and Christianity emerged with close ties to the land.

Archaeology

Dalia notices a silver plaque inscribed with the Priestly Blessing in ancient Hebrew script. The plaque was discovered at an archaeological site near Jerusalem. Israel is loaded with artifacts that reveal its long and rich history. How incredible it would be, Dalia considers, if she were to dig up something so old and so historically significant. Maybe she'll be an archaeologist someday.

▲ **Archaeologists** uncover artifacts of earlier cultures that have become buried over time, such as tools, pottery, or wall paintings.

◄ Remains of the ancient fortress at **Masada**, where Jewish rebels are believed to have held out against the Roman army until their defeat in 73 CE.

archaeological treasures

► In the second century BCE, the Greeks outlawed all Jewish religious practices and desecrated the Second Temple, until a Jew named Judah Maccabee led a revolt. We remember this story when we light **Ḥanukkah candles**.

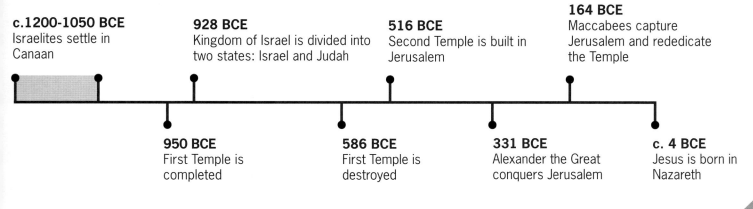

c.1200-1050 BCE
Israelites settle in Canaan

928 BCE
Kingdom of Israel is divided into two states: Israel and Judah

516 BCE
Second Temple is built in Jerusalem

164 BCE
Maccabees capture Jerusalem and rededicate the Temple

950 BCE
First Temple is completed

586 BCE
First Temple is destroyed

331 BCE
Alexander the Great conquers Jerusalem

c. 4 BCE
Jesus is born in Nazareth

Diaspora

Inside the museum, Dalia and her friends walk through reconstructed synagogues from India, Germany, and Italy. They see Havdalah spice boxes from Austria, seder plates from Spain, Ḥanukkah lamps from Italy, and much more. After the Romans destroyed the Second Temple in 70 CE the Jewish people dispersed around the world, forming new communities in Persia (now Iran), Syria, Egypt, Babylonia (now Iraq), and even India.

At different points in history, groups of Jews made aliyah to Israel, but the vast majority lived in the Diaspora outside of Israel. They continued to study Torah, observe Jewish tradition, and express their longing for the Land of Israel. As the centuries passed, each Diaspora community developed unique customs, styles of clothing, and even languages, such as Yiddish in Eastern Europe and Ladino, spoken by Jews of Spanish origin. Meanwhile, the Land of Israel became home to many other civilizations, especially the Arabs, who brought with them the religion of Islam, based on the teachings of the prophet Muhammad.

▲ **Torah cover** from Amersterdam, 1771

Early immigration

As Jewish communities across Europe suffered persecution and even expulsion from countries like England (1290) and Spain (1492), more and more Jews returned to Palestine, as the Land of Israel was then called. These new immigrants added considerably to the Jewish population already there.

The first wave of mass immigration to Israel, known as the **First Aliyah**, began in 1882, following **pogroms** (organized attacks on Jews) in Russia. At that time, Palestine was under the rule of the Ottoman Turks. Over the next twenty years, around 35,000 Jews moved to Palestine, mostly from Eastern Europe, as the goal of creating a Jewish state took hold. Many of these pioneers established farming communities, where they struggled to survive despite poverty, disease, and lack of agricultural experience.

An early **pioneer** working on the farm ▶

◀ The Great Synagogue in the once-thriving Jewish community of Pilsen, **Czech Republic**

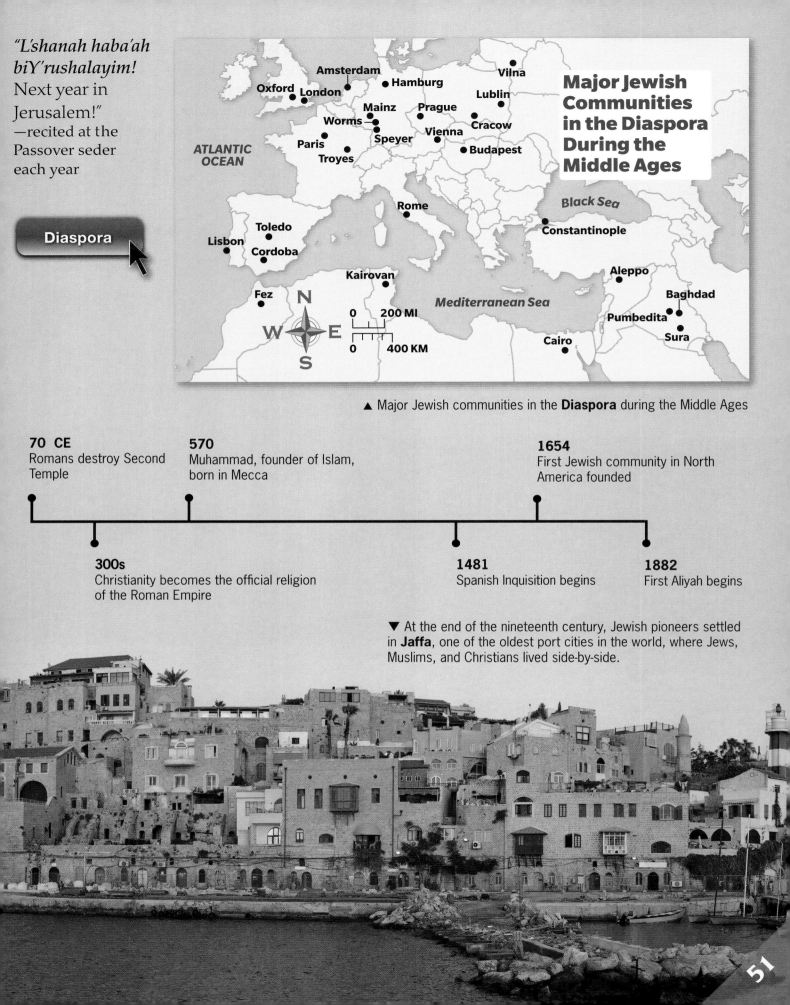

"L'shanah haba'ah biY'rushalayim! Next year in Jerusalem!"
—recited at the Passover seder each year

Diaspora

Major Jewish Communities in the Diaspora During the Middle Ages

Oxford
Amsterdam
London
Hamburg
Vilna
Lublin
Mainz
Prague
Worms
Cracow
Speyer
Vienna
Paris
Budapest
Troyes
ATLANTIC OCEAN
Rome
Black Sea
Constantinople
Toledo
Lisbon
Cordoba
Aleppo
Kairovan
Baghdad
Fez
Pumbedita
Mediterranean Sea
Sura
Cairo
N W E S
0   200 MI
0   400 KM

▲ Major Jewish communities in the **Diaspora** during the Middle Ages

70 CE
Romans destroy Second Temple

570
Muhammad, founder of Islam, born in Mecca

1654
First Jewish community in North America founded

300s
Christianity becomes the official religion of the Roman Empire

1481
Spanish Inquisition begins

1882
First Aliyah begins

▼ At the end of the nineteenth century, Jewish pioneers settled in **Jaffa**, one of the oldest port cities in the world, where Jews, Muslims, and Christians lived side-by-side.

Zionism

In 1895, a young Hungarian Jewish journalist named Theodor Herzl was assigned to report on a breaking news story. Captain Alfred Dreyfus, a French Jew, was wrongly accused of spying on France. His trial and conviction, known as the **Dreyfus Affair**, was grossly unjust and openly anti-Semitic. In response to the hatred Herzl witnessed, he wrote a book called *The Jewish State*, arguing that anti-Semitism would end only if the Jews had their own land.

Herzl's idea sparked great excitement and, in 1897, Herzl held the First Zionist Congress in Switzerland, bringing together approximately 200 representatives from 17 countries to adopt his plan of founding a Jewish state. "If you will it, it is no dream," Herzl proclaimed.

Herzl has been called the father of Zionism for his role in spearheading the movement to establish and support a Jewish State in the Land of Israel.

▲ Theodor Herzl

Zionism

▼ **Kibbutz members** picking oranges, 1938

The kibbutz

Between 1904 and 1914, another 40,000 Jews came to Palestine in a wave of immigration called the **Second Aliyah**, mostly fleeing pogroms and increasing anti-Semitism in Russia. A group of these young Eastern European pioneers founded the first **kibbutz** (communal settlement) in 1909, called Deganyah. They were motivated by Zionist ideals of returning to the Jewish homeland and a commitment to hard work and social equality.

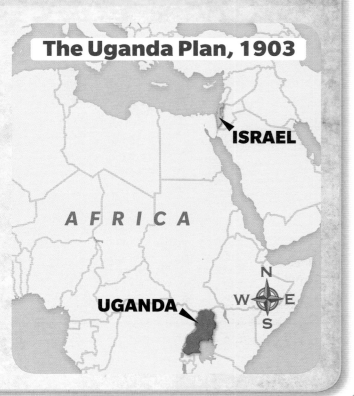

▲ The **founding fathers** of Tel Aviv. The bustling city of Tel Aviv is just over 100 years old. It was founded by Jewish pioneers on the outskirts of the ancient city of Jaffa (or Yafo) in 1909. The combined city is now called Tel Aviv-Jaffa.

1895
Alfred Dreyfus convicted of spying

1904
Second Aliyah begins

1897
First Zionist Congress held in Switzerland

1909
First kibbutz is founded

The original *kibbutzim* (plural of kibbutz) were agricultural collectives. All the members worked together to run the farm, sharing all their food, property, and resources. Kibbutz members ate all their meals in communal dining halls and earned wages based on their needs, not on their status or job title.

DEBATE IT

The Zionist goal had always been to create a Jewish state in the Land of Israel. But the Ottoman Empire rulers were not interested in giving up Palestine. With European Jews in constant danger of pogroms, the matter took on new urgency, and so, in 1903, Herzl decided to consider the Uganda Plan, a British offer of land in East Africa. A state for the Jews, even in Uganda, would provide an immediate safe haven from violence. But many Zionists believed that the only way to ensure the survival of the Jewish people and culture was to return to the Jewish homeland, the Land of Israel.

Imagine you are at the Sixth Zionist Congress and the Uganda Plan is being debated. Would you support a new Jewish homeland in East Africa? Would you only accept a Jewish homeland in the Land of Israel? Why?

Have a debate.

UGANDA PLAN vs **ONLY IN ISRAEL**

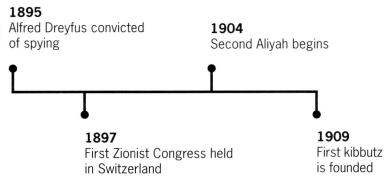

The Uganda Plan, 1903

ISRAEL

AFRICA

UGANDA

N W E S

Emerging conflict

When the British army defeated the Turks in World War I, Palestine, home to Arabs and Jews, came under British rule. Britain's **Balfour Declaration** in 1917 promised support for a Jewish homeland in Palestine. Many Arabs living in Palestine, however, opposed the idea of Jewish immigration. They wanted an Arab state in Palestine, and had been led to believe they had British support.

As wave after wave of Jews immigrated to the Land of Israel, the Jewish population grew, and Jewish settlers increasingly bought up Arab land. Riots and revolts flared up in the 1920s and 1930s as Arabs reacted with anger and fear of being displaced by Jewish development. In response, Jews formed militias, such as the **Haganah** and Irgun, to defend their communities from Arab violence.

"His Majesty's Government view with favour the establishment in Palestine of a national home for the Jewish people...."
—from the Balfour Declaration, 1917

▲ The Zionist leader **Chaim Weizmann** convinced the British to issue the Balfour Declaration. He later served as Israel's first president.

British response

In 1937, determined to put an end to escalating street fights between Arabs and Jews, a British commission recommended dividing Palestine into two states—one Arab, one Jewish. But the Arabs rejected it—they wanted an Arab state that included all of Palestine.

◄ Young Arab men **rioting** in response to Jewish immigration.

1914-1918
World War I

1920
Haganah formed to protect Jews of Palestine

1939
Britain's White Paper restricts Jewish immigration to Palestine

1917
Balfour Declaration promises support for a Jewish homeland

1933
Adolf Hitler becomes chancellor of Germany

1939
World War II begins

In the meantime, World War II was brewing in Europe, and the British decided they needed Arab support to defeat Germany. So in 1939, Britain issued the **White Paper**, an official government report declaring that Palestine was to be an independent state. To ensure an Arab majority, Britain severely restricted Jewish immigration to Palestine and the sale of land to Jews.

Now the dream of a Jewish state in Palestine was even further from reach, just as Adolf Hitler's rise to power threatened the Jewish populations of Germany and the rest of Europe. The Jews in Palestine were furious with the British, but they needed to ally themselves with Britain to help defeat Hitler. So, despite their anger, thousands of Jews living in Palestine joined the British military, produced weapons and supplies for the British, and contributed to the fight against the Nazis.

▲ Jewish youth protesting the British **White Paper** in Tel Aviv, 1939

"We shall fight the war as if there were no White Paper and we shall fight the White Paper as if there were no war."

—David Ben-Gurion

Jewish women volunteers in the British Auxiliary Territorial Service, 1942 ▶

The Holocaust

By 1944, the horrific magnitude of the Nazi atrocities of the Holocaust was coming to light—the gas chambers; death camps; and the "final solution," Hitler's plan to kill all the Jews in Europe. Six million Jews were murdered in the Holocaust, and hundreds of thousands of survivors became displaced persons (DPs, or refugees), with nowhere to go and little or no family left.

Displaced persons

With anti-Semitism still strong in Europe, many survivors who tried to return to their former villages after the war found that they weren't welcome. At the same time, the British enforced their White Paper and refused to let displaced Jews into Palestine. The Haganah tried smuggling in refugees, but 90 percent of their ships were stopped by the British. Britain decided to turn the problem over to the United Nations (the UN).

◀ Illegal **Jewish immigrants** being deported by British soldiers, from the Haifa port to Cyprus, 1947

Partition Plan

A special UN committee recommended another partition plan—dividing Palestine into separate Jewish and Arab states. Zionists accepted the plan, happy at the prospect of having an independent Jewish state and control over immigration. The Arabs argued that they weren't given a fair portion of the land, since they numbered twice as many as the Jews but would get less than half of Palestine. Despite Arab threats of war, the UN General Assembly voted in favor of the **Partition Plan** in November 1947, and the British prepared to pack their bags.

▲ The **United Nations** votes in favor of partition.

Statehood!

On the morning of May 14, 1948, the British left. That very afternoon, Jewish leaders gathered in Tel Aviv as David Ben-Gurion stood under a picture of Theodor Herzl and read the stirring words of Israel's Declaration of Independence, establishing the newborn State of Israel. The crowd spontaneously sang "Hatikvah," but there was little time for celebration. The very next day, five of Israel's neighbors—Egypt, Syria, Transjordan (now called Jordan), Lebanon, and Iraq— attacked the one-day-old Jewish state.

▶ **David Ben-Gurion** first set foot in the Land of Israel in 1906, as part of the Second Aliyah. He picked oranges and helped establish the first agricultural workers' group that later evolved into the first kibbutz. Ben-Gurion oversaw military operations during the War of Independence, and became the state's first prime minister.

▶ "We, members of the people's council, representatives of the Jewish community of Eretz Yisrael and of the Zionist movement. . . by virtue of our natural and historic right and on the strength of the resolution of the United Nations General Assembly, hereby declare the establishment of a Jewish state in Eretz Yisrael, to be known as the State of Israel."
—from Israel's Declaration of Independence

A PLACE TO CALL HOME

With the founding of the State of Israel, the Jewish people finally had a place to call home, a safe haven following the Holocaust, a land where all Jews could practice Judaism without fear. What do you think it means to be a Zionist now that the State of Israel exists?

▲ Israelis celebrate the UN vote on partition, 1947

Declaration of Independence

1948 Establishment of modern State of Israel

1945
World War II ends

1947 UN General Assembly votes to partition Palestine into Jewish and Arab states

War of Independence

As the bus travels along the Jerusalem-Tel Aviv highway, Dalia snaps photos out the window. Lining the road are burnt-out skeletons of armored vehicles, left here as a monument to Israel's fight for independence.

The **War of Independence** was brutal for both sides, and many lives were lost in the intense fighting. But Israel's soldiers were well organized and well trained, and they won that first war. By the time the fighting ended, Israel controlled more territory than it would have had under the Partition Plan. Transjordan controlled the West Bank and East Jerusalem, including the Old City, and Egypt controlled the Gaza Strip.

The Israeli army had triumphed over much larger Arab armies, the Zionist dream of a Jewish homeland was finally realized, and nations around the world recognized Israel's right to exist.

▲ An Israeli soldier guards a police station during the **War of Independence.**

1948-49
War of Independence

1948-52
Israel's population doubles

Palestinian refugees

But what Israel calls the War of Independence, Palestinians call *Nakba*, meaning "catastrophe." Approximately 700,000 Palestinian Arabs left their homes and became refugees. Some left before the war, others left at the urging of Arab leaders who warned them to get out of the way of advancing armies, and still others were forced to leave. Israel did not allow most of the Palestinian refugees to return after the war, out of concern that they would not support the Jewish state.

▶ As the Zionist founders of Israel built schools and synagogues, founded universities and hospitals, and planted trees in the desert, the modern State of Israel restored the pride and strength of a battered Jewish people.

Many of those who fled became refugees in the territories known as the West Bank and Gaza Strip. The neighboring Arab countries refused to resettle the Palestinians in their countries, placing them in refugee camps instead. Only Jordan offered them citizenship. The 150,000 Arabs who remained in Israel, however, were granted citizenship in the new state.

▲ Immigrants arrived faster than homes could be built and so **ma'abarot, refugee camps**, crowded with tents and other temporary dwellings, were set up to accommodate the masses. Over time, the *ma'abarot* were absorbed into neighboring towns or became towns of their own, with permanent dwellings.

Israel Survives

Territory under the U.N. Partition Plan:
- Jewish
- Arab
- International authority
- Israel's borders after the War of Independence

LEBANON
SYRIA
Haifa
Tel Aviv
Jericho
Mediterranean Sea
Jerusalem
Gaza
Dead Sea
ISRAEL
NEGEV DESERT
EGYPT
JORDAN

N W E S

0   30 MI
0   30 KM

Population explosion

With the war over, Israel's top priority became absorbing the waves of Jewish immigrants pouring into the country. Almost 700,000 immigrants arrived during Israel's first three years of existence, doubling its population to more than 1.3 million. Half were Holocaust survivors from Europe. The other half were Jewish refugees from Arab countries in the Middle East and North Africa who faced persecution due to Arab-Israeli tension following the War of Independence. With their collective lifestyle, kibbutzim were well suited to absorbing new arrivals, and they grew rapidly. By 1950 there were more than 67,000 kibbutz members in Israel. By 1967, Israel would again double in population.

◄ As a result of Israel's **War of Independence**, its borders expanded.

immigration

Fighting for survival

At the Israeli Museum at the Yitzḥak Rabin Center in Tel Aviv, a powerful film introduces Dalia and her classmates to footage of the **Six-Day War**. After the War of Independence, Israel's Arab neighbors remained hostile to the Jewish state. In the 1956 Suez Campaign, Israel and Egypt clashed over important shipping routes through the Suez Canal and the Straits of Tiran. The peace that followed was broken in 1967, in the Six-Day War, when Egypt once again blocked the Straits of Tiran to Israeli ships. In response, Israel launched a surprise air attack against Egypt. Jordan and Syria joined the war on Egypt's side but were quickly defeated.

New territories

As a result of the Six-Day War, Israel gained new territories, including the Golan Heights (from Syria), the Sinai Peninsula and Gaza Strip (from Egypt), and the West Bank and East Jerusalem (from Jordan). These territories tripled Israel's size and provided added security, since rockets launched from Egypt and Syria could no longer reach major cities in Israel. And Jews finally had access to the Old City of Jerusalem, which Jordan had controlled since 1948. Jews could once again visit their holiest site, the Kotel.

Jewish settlements

At first, Jewish settlement in the new territories was limited. But by the late 1970s, the Israeli government began to encourage these settlements, especially in the West Bank, to help serve as a buffer between Israel and the Palestinian territories.

The United States, along with other countries and the UN, argues that Jewish settlements in the disputed territories make peace negotiations with the Arabs more difficult, because future peace agreements are likely to require Israeli withdrawal from at least some of the territories. As of 2009, close to 280,000 Jews lived in 121 West Bank settlements.

▼ The **Jewish settlement Ma'aleh Adumim** was established in the West Bank in 1977 as a commuter town for residents working in nearby Jerusalem.

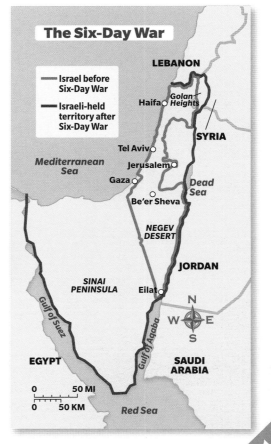

LIVING JEWISH VALUES:
זִכָּרוֹן *Zikaron*, Remembrance

On **Yom Hazikaron**, Israel's Memorial Day, air raid sirens bring the State of Israel to a complete stop. Drivers pull over and stand at attention for a full two minutes. All movie theaters and clubs are closed, and radio and TV broadcasts focus on fallen Israeli soldiers. It's a somber day of remembrance.

Then, as the sun sets, Yom Hazikaron gives way to **Yom Ha'atzma'ut**, Israel Independence Day, joyfully celebrated with parades, barbecues, and Israeli flags everywhere. The two days are joined to make it clear: Israelis owe the very existence of their country to the people—more than 26,000 of them—who gave their lives for it.

War and a peace treaty

In 1973, on Yom Kippur, the holiest day of the Jewish year, Egypt and Syria launched a surprise attack against Israel. At first, Israel was caught off guard and outnumbered. Casualties in the **Yom Kippur War** were high, but Israel triumphed and the war ended less than a month later with a ceasefire.

President Anwar al-Sadat visited Israel in 1977 in the first public show of friendship from an Arab state. Two years later, Israel and Egypt signed a peace treaty, in which Israel agreed to return the Sinai Peninsula to Egypt.

◀ **Egyptian President Anwar al-Sadat** addressed the Knesset in Jerusalem in 1977, "I declare to the whole world that we accept to live with you in a permanent peace based on justice."

The Six-Day War

— Israel before Six-Day War

— Israeli-held territory after Six-Day War

LEBANON
Golan Heights
Haifa
Mediterranean Sea
SYRIA
Tel Aviv
Jerusalem
Gaza
Dead Sea
Be'er Sheva
NEGEV DESERT
JORDAN
SINAI PENINSULA
Eilat
Gulf of Suez
Gulf of Aqaba
EGYPT
SAUDI ARABIA
Red Sea

0   50 MI
0   50 KM

1956
Suez Campaign

1973
Yom Kippur War

1967
Six-Day War

1979
Israel and Egypt sign peace treaty

▶ The area under Israeli control expanded as a result of the **Six-Day War**.

Continuing conflict

Arabs in the West Bank and Gaza Strip grew increasingly angry at the Israeli presence and settlements in the territories. In 1987, Palestinian rage exploded in an uprising called the **Intifada** (Arabic for "shaking off"), which would last for six years. Rioting and rock-throwing escalated into attacks with homemade explosives and guns.

Striving for peace

In 1993, hopes for finally achieving peace were high with the signing of the Oslo Accords. Palestinian leader Yasir Arafat, the chairman of the **Palestine Liberation Organization**, or **PLO**, for many years, and the first president of the Palestinian National Authority, renounced terrorism and recognized Israel's right to exist. In return, Israel's Prime Minister Yitzhak Rabin agreed to extend self-rule to the Palestinians in the Gaza Strip and parts of the West Bank.

▼ **Palestinian rioters** near Ramallah, 2000

Despite the agreement, tensions were high. In 1995, Rabin was assassinated by a Jewish extremist who opposed the peace process. U.S. President Bill Clinton brought both sides together in 2000 with renewed hopes of negotiating a lasting peace agreement. But Arafat rejected the proposed compromise, and the territories broke out once again in violence.

▲ **Yasir Arafat** giving a speech at the White House after the signing of the Oslo Accords

Escalating violence

The **Second Intifada** brought the violence into the heart of Israel, with horrific suicide bombings targeting Israeli soldiers and civilians alike. Israel responded with counterattacks and in 2002 began building a security fence to separate the territories from the rest of Israel.

Disengagement

Two years later, as the violence began to quiet down, Yasir Arafat died, removing what many Israelis saw as an obstacle to peace. In 2005, Israeli Prime Minister Ariel Sharon turned over the Gaza Strip and part of the West Bank to the Palestinians, in an effort to advance the peace process. He pulled the Israeli army out and evicted Jewish settlers from more than twenty settlements.

But the **Disengagement Plan** didn't bring peace. A fundamentalist Islamic group called **Hamas** won the Palestinian elections in Gaza in 2006, winning support for their promises of medical care, schools, and other services. But Hamas is a terrorist group committed to destroying Israel. Soon Hamas began firing rockets into Israel from Gaza, repeatedly hitting nearby Israeli towns, such as S'derot.

▲ Remains of some of the thousands of rockets fired on **S'derot** from the Gaza Strip

Continued efforts

World leaders continue their efforts to bring peace to the region. A proposed two-state solution envisions the creation of a Palestinian state alongside Israel, which would remain a Jewish state. Israelis are concerned, though, that Palestinians won't accept Israel's existence on any terms. Security is a constant concern in Israel, and peace so far remains an elusive goal.

The future

The history of Israel continues to unfold. Jews around the world make aliyah. The peace process develops. Arabs and Jews clash and also learn how to live side by side. Dalia decides she wants to be a photojournalist—to capture the important moments in history that are yet to come.

BACK TO THE SOURCES

"They will beat their swords into plowshares and their spears into pruning hooks; nation will not lift sword against nation, and they will no longer study warfare." —Isaiah 2:4

Rewrite this quote in your own words. _____

In small groups, brainstorm three steps you would take toward peace if you were in charge.

Write letters to your local representative and to the prime minister of Israel to convince them of your ideas.

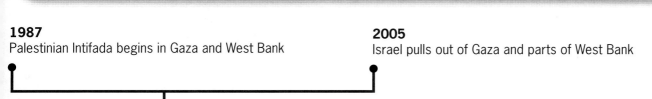

1987
Palestinian Intifada begins in Gaza and West Bank

2005
Israel pulls out of Gaza and parts of West Bank

2000 Second Intifada begins

6 SECURITY AND CONFLICT
In the Headlines

Twice a month, thousands gather at the Kotel plaza in Jerusalem to watch the induction of new soldiers into combat units of the Israel Defense Forces (IDF), or Tzahal. These 18-year-olds have endured months of basic training in which they've conducted countless drills under the sweltering sun, marched almost 25 miles carrying heavy packs and weapons, and lived for a week in the field. Now they stand in straight rows, knowing the security, integrity, and strength of the country is in their hands. Security is a constant concern in this tiny country that has experienced more than its share of bloodshed.

"I swear and obligate myself on my word of honor to remain loyal to the State of Israel, its laws and its authorities…to obey all commands and orders given by authorized commanders [of the IDF], and to devote all my strength, and even sacrifice my life, in the defense of the homeland and the freedom of Israel."
— from the IDF's oath of allegiance

IDF

▲ **IDF soldiers** at the Kotel

Society and the army

Because army duty is compulsory, the army is more than a defensive body for the country; the swearing-in ceremony is an important rite of passage for young Israelis, and the army itself provides an important social network. Whether they are rich or poor, recent immigrants or sabras, Israelis from all walks of life serve their country together. Unit members, who spend two to three years depending on one another, often form close bonds. Even after active duty, they often reunite in reserves and thus maintain close friendships throughout their lives. Many jobs are only open to army veterans, and veterans get special benefits from the government.

ALTERNATIVES TO THE ARMY

The rule is that every able-bodied Israeli must serve in the army, but every rule has its exceptions. For example, religiously observant Jewish women, Arab Israelis, and yeshiva students are excused from serving in the IDF.

Many people who are exempt from IDF service still want to serve their country. **Sherut Leumi (National Service)** is a program in which 18- to 21-year-olds perform community work instead of military service. These volunteers are sent to schools, hospitals, or nursing homes where they might help immigrants or teens at risk, or serve poor communities—similar to AmeriCorps in the United States or Canada World Youth.

Design a flyer encouraging those exempted from the army to sign up for Sherut Leumi. Consider:

Why should they serve their country?

How does working in a school or hospital help the State of Israel?

What might the volunteer gain personally from doing Sherut Leumi?

▲ A volunteer tutors a Sudanese immigrant.

Drafted

In the shadow of unresolved conflicts with the Palestinians, Uri, a teen living in Jerusalem, is preparing to join the IDF. Now that he's 18, he's been drafted. Israel is the only country in the world in which both men and women are required to serve—men for three years, and women for two. Afterward, they continue to serve for a few weeks a year in the reserves.

Uri is on his way to take the physical, psychological, and written exams that will determine where he will be assigned. If the results show he's capable and in tip-top shape, he'll be assigned a prestigious—and probably dangerous—job. Like many of his friends, he dreams about being a paratrooper, even though the idea of parachuting out of an airplane is terrifying.

▲ **IDF soldiers** in the West Bank

Border security

On the bus, Uri's mind wanders to other jobs he might have in the army. If he joins the Armored Corps, Uri could learn to drive a tank. Those huge combat vehicles are the first line of attack during a war, and in peacetime they're used as mobile bunkers to perform various security duties, like patrolling Israel's borders.

Because Israel is bordered by hostile neighbors, border security is crucial. In Lebanon, the terrorist group **Hezbollah** is dedicated to destroying the State of Israel. Meanwhile, Syria is in a dispute with Israel over ownership of the Golan Heights. The borders with Egypt and Jordan are jointly maintained with those countries, which are at peace with Israel.

▼ A tank on patrol in the **Golan Heights**.

Security fence

In 2002, during the Second Intifada, the Israeli government started building a barrier to separate much of the West Bank from Israel and prevent terrorists from entering the country. A portion of the fence was built just a few miles from Uri's home.

▲ **Hezbollah's flag**

The barrier succeeded in preventing attacks; however, it has provoked controversy because it was built in part on land owned or claimed by Palestinians. Opponents also argue that the barrier makes it harder for Palestinian civilians to get to jobs, schools, and hospitals in Israel; limits their access to water, a crucial resource; and even separates some people's homes from their fields and animal flocks. Israel's Supreme Court ruled that Israel has a right to build a fence to protect its citizens but has to balance the need for security with the impact of the fence on people living along its route.

▲ Portions of the **security barrier** between Israel and the West Bank. In a region where even names can be controversial, Israelis commonly call it a "security fence," while Palestinians often call it a "segregation wall."

security fence

Checkpoints

If Uri joins the Military Police Corps, he might end up manning a checkpoint. To prevent terrorists from entering Israel, Israel built checkpoints throughout the territories, where soldiers inspect travelers and vehicles for weapons and explosives. Weapons have been found hidden in rolled-up prayer rugs, and explosives in ambulances, and so everything—absolutely everything—must be thoroughly checked.

▲ An Israeli soldier searches a car at a checkpoint in Bethlehem.

▲ A boy in Gaza

Life in the territories

More than three million Arabs live in the territories that Israel captured during the 1967 Six-Day War, the vast majority in the West Bank. Unemployment and poverty rates are high, in part because Israeli border security makes it difficult for many Palestinians to travel to jobs, and leads to shortages of food, medicine, and fuel.

In recent years there have been signs of economic improvement in the West Bank, such as the 2009 opening of the first movie theater in Nablus in twenty years, and the 2010 appearance of dozens of busy new restaurants and juice bars in Ramallah. With improved security, Israel has been able to reduce the number of checkpoints in the West Bank, making life a little easier for residents.

Responding to attacks

Uri's classmate Ziv boards the bus. Ziv joined the class in 2005 after the Disengagement, when Ziv's family and community were forced to leave their settlement in the Gaza Strip. In an effort to stop the rocket attacks from the Gaza Strip that followed Israel's pullout, in December 2008 Israel launched air strikes, followed by a ground assault. It destroyed various Hamas targets in Gaza that were the base for the attacks, but also destroyed private homes and schools.

▶ Name one fact that relates to Israel's security challenges or recent history for each of the places marked on this map.

Israel and its Neighbors

LEBANON

SYRIA

Golan Heights

Mediterranean Sea

West Bank

Jerusalem

Gaza

Dead Sea

JORDAN

EGYPT

Gulf of Suez

Gulf of Aqaba

Red Sea

N W E S

0   50 MI
0   50 KM

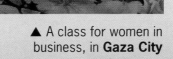
▲ A class for women in business, in **Gaza City**

▼ A city in the **West Bank**

▲ Smoke rises from Gaza after an Israeli air strike against Hamas missile-launching sites.

In addition, Israel imposed a blockade on goods entering the region. Humanitarian aid was allowed, but Israel blocked almost everything else, including steel, pipes, and building equipment that could be used to make weapons. However, the more than four thousand homes that were reportedly destroyed by Israel in its 2008 air strikes cannot be rebuilt without these materials, and thousands of Palestinians remained homeless. The water and sewer system in Gaza, as well as electricity networks, were damaged; they also require supplies in order to be repaired.

There are no easy answers to the conflict. Israel needs to defend itself from Palestinian violence, and seeks to balance security with the humanitarian needs of the territories.

MEET A PALESTINIAN

Rami, age 17, is an Arab teen from Beit Tzafafa, in East Jerusalem. He is active in a group called Sulhita which brings together Muslim, Christian, and Jewish youth—people like him who believe in working towards peace. Activities as varied as horseback riding or his favorite, Capoeira (a type of Brazilian martial arts combined with dance and music), let young people from different backgrounds share common interests.

"I try to do sulha (Arabic for mediation), every day by talking to people, trying to convince them we are all humans and what's important is what's inside the person," says Rami.

A Muslim, Rami says his parents have always had Christian, Muslim, and Jewish friends and he grew up with the value of respecting all types of people. "Sometimes when I talk to people about this they may yell at me or be afraid of me, but I think there is a key to every person's heart, if we can just find the key and open them up."

▲ An **unattended bag** may look harmless, but Israelis have learned to be cautious.

Day-to-day security

An unattended shopping bag on Uri's bus has caused quite a stir. The bus driver asks everyone to evacuate the bus just in case the bag contains something dangerous. Uri is used to this kind of thing and just hopes it won't take too long.

Because security is top priority, Israelis are extra careful. For example, there are guards checking bags at the entrance to most public buildings, banks, and department stores; public buses that travel through areas of conflict are bullet-proof; and Israelis are cautious about bags left unattended on crowded buses, sidewalks, or park benches. Having served in the army or reserves, most Israelis are trained to help in an emergency, and many even carry weapons. The shopping bag turns out to be harmless, and the bus finally settles down and continues on its way.

Airport safety

As a plane passes overhead, Uri's thoughts turn to the sky. Joining the Air Force would mean that Uri could learn how to fly. Fighter pilots often go on to fly for regular airlines after active duty. Israel's Ben-Gurion International Airport is considered the safest airport in the world, hands-down. Security officials—in uniform and plainclothes—patrol the airport at all times. They talk with each passenger and look for suspicious behavior, body language, and anything else that doesn't seem right.

▲ Many civilians own **gas masks** to protect against the threat of chemical or biological weapons.

◀ A **security guard** checks bags at the entrance to the Dizengoff Center, a shopping mall in Tel Aviv.

▼ No flight out of **Ben-Gurion International Airport** has ever been hijacked.

Intelligence

If Uri doesn't fly for the Air Force, he might find a cool job on the ground, like intelligence. Aman is the intelligence branch of the IDF. They collect information, evaluate security threats, and try to learn other countries' secrets.

In addition to Aman, Israel's intelligence community also includes the Mossad, which does overseas intelligence work, including pursuing terrorists and sharing intelligence with friendly countries, and the Shin Bet, which is responsible for exposing terrorist rings within the country, protecting important public officials, and keeping Israeli airlines safe. Uri can already picture himself as a spy with a fake mustache and a trench coat.

After taking his profile tests, at long last Uri sits across from his IDF interviewer. Drum roll please.... Uri has earned a very respectable 64 (out of 97) and opts to join the army police intelligence force. No trench coat or pilot's wings, but exciting and important all the same.

airport security

▲ **Soldiers** are a familiar sight on the streets of Israel.

DEBATE IT

Hawks and doves are birds, yes, but these terms are also used to describe people based on their political views. For a hawk, named after the predatory bird, military strength is often the means to peace and security, while a dove is more likely to look first to negotiation and compromise for peaceful ways to resolve a conflict.

In Israeli politics, doves endorse the strategy of returning portions of the disputed territories to the Palestinians in exchange for peace. The most successful example of land for peace occurred in 1979, when Israel returned the Sinai Peninsula to Egypt and signed a historic peace agreement. Hawks, on the other hand, maintain that secure borders are essential to Israel's existence; therefore, they are reluctant to return land seized on the West Bank and Gaza during the Six-Day War in 1967. Should Israel compromise and give up land for the sake of peace? Have a debate.

LAND FOR PEACE vs DEMONSTRATE STRENGTH

What other solution can you think of?

Military ethics

One of the most important things Uri will learn in the army is the Israeli military ethical code. Ethics play a big role in Israel's military. Any army must balance its nation's security needs with humanitarian concerns and the need to protect civilians. It's especially important in Israel, where the terrorist organization Hamas tends to hide among civilians and deliberately place its equipment and fighters in places like schools and hospitals.

In fact, the Israeli army's official ethical code emphasizes the sanctity of human life and each soldier's obligation to act morally and ethically. Living according to these values can come at a significant cost, sometimes requiring soldiers to put their own lives at greater risk in order to avoid harming civilians on either side of the conflict, but the IDF is committed to its code of values based on Jewish tradition, democratic principles, and its military heritage.

▼ Israeli soldier **Gilad Shalit** was captured by Hamas in 2006. Israelis demonstrate in 2009 for his release.

DEBATE IT

There are many conflicting opinions when it comes to Israeli security issues, from settlements to checkpoints, exceptions to military service, prisoner exchanges, and more. We can respect each other's opinions, even when we disagree.

<u>Underline</u> all the potential debate topics you can find in this chapter, then discuss your viewpoints on these issues with your classmates. How does it feel to disagree with each other about Israel's actions? Brainstorm ways to respond to conflicting viewpoints held by classmates, friends, family members, or even the media.

YOUR TURN: MILITARY SERVICE

When Uri graduates from high school, he's headed straight for the IDF. College will wait until after his three years of service are finished.

What would you like to do after high school?

_____

_____

Imagine that you were required to do army service. What job in the military would you choose? Why?

_____

_____

▲ Women cadets taking part in infantry training

American role

Although America doesn't always agree with Israel's policies and actions, the United States is one of Israel's most important allies and shows its support with financial, military, and diplomatic aid. The U.S. recognizes that Israel is the only democratic nation in the Middle East, and the two countries work together to fight terrorism.

▲ Yasir Arafat, Shimon Peres, and Yitzhak Rabin display their Nobel Peace Prizes.

▲ U.S. President Bill Clinton (center) hosted peace talks between Israeli Prime Minister Ehud Barak (left) and Palestinian leader Yasir Arafat (right) at Camp David in 2000.

American presidents have initiated and moderated many of the peace negotiations between Israel and neighboring countries, including the Camp David Accords between Israel and Egypt (1978), the Oslo Accords between Israel and the Palestine Liberation Organization (1993), and the Israel-Jordan peace treaty (1994). Unfortunately, peace negotiations between Israel and Syria have failed, Israel and Lebanon are far from peace, and agreements with the Palestinians have repeatedly broken down.

American allies

Building peace

Continued negotiations between Israel, Palestinian leaders, and the world community seek to establish lasting peace in the Middle East. Israel is at peace with Jordan and Egypt. PLO chairman Yasir Arafat, Israeli Foreign Minister Shimon Peres, and Israeli Prime Minister Yitzhak Rabin together won the Nobel Peace Prize in 1994 for their efforts toward peace in the region. But there's much work to be done to ensure a peaceful, secure future in which Israelis and Palestinians can live side-by-side in harmony.

▲ The signing ceremony for the **Israel-Jordan peace treaty**, 1994

CREATIVE DIALOGUE

Here are some of the many organizations that bring people together in creative ways to encourage dialogue for peace.

▼ **Peace Child Israel** provides Jewish and Arab teens the opportunity to write and produce an original play that highlights how they experience the Arab-Israeli conflict. To do this, they need to get to know each other and overcome stereotypes. The program culminates in live performances that bring the message of tolerance to mixed audiences of Jews and Arabs.

▲ **Twinned Peace & Sport Schools** of the Peres Center for Peace is an afterschool program for Israeli and Palestinian kids who come together for sporting and social activities. Whether on the soccer field or the basketball court, kids learn to accept cultural differences and break down negative stereotypes while improving sports skills and having fun.

▶ In the United States, **Seeds of Peace International Camp,** located at Pleasant Lake in Maine, brings together teens from areas in conflict around the world, including Israeli and Palestinian teens, for three weeks of canoeing, basketball, and color games, as well as dialogue about war and peace. The hope is that when teens from different cultures meet in a neutral setting, free from the pressures and prejudices of home, they discover common ground, break down barriers of mistrust, and open the door to friendship, reconciliation, and coexistence. Plant a seed of friendship, and you've got a shot at growing peace.

What do each of these programs have in common? Why do you think the programs are targeted at kids? Look for programs that promote peace and understanding in other chapters of this book.

7 THE ENVIRONMENT
The Great Outdoors

Visit Israel and the scenery is sure to take your breath away. In the Galilee region to the north, you'll find beautiful mountains, waterfalls, and fields of wildflowers as far as the eye can see. On the Mediterranean coast, you'll encounter sandy beaches and the incredible expanses of the open sea. Further south, in the Negev, expect to see massive sand dunes and desert animals such as ibex, hyenas, and gazelles grazing among the barren rocks and desert springs. And on farms around the country you'll glimpse fields of oranges, dates, and wheat. Israel has a wide array of beautiful landscapes and natural resources.

Environmental challenges

Sound idyllic? Well, in many ways it is. However, pollution, water shortages, and other environmental concerns have taken their toll on nature in Israel, as they have throughout the world. About 98 percent of water flow from the lower part of the Jordan River has been diverted for agricultural and personal use by Israel and neighboring countries, and air pollution in Tel Aviv continues to be a significant problem.

▶ In a land area roughly the size of New Jersey, Israel has marine landscapes, sand dunes, farms, craters, mountains, and more. The country has nearly 200 nature reserves, dozens of national parks, and hundreds of protected plants and species.

nature tour

Salt builds up along the shore of the **Dead Sea**, which is shrinking because of decreased water flow coming from the Jordan river. ▶

JUDAISM AND THE ENVIRONMENT

▲ Celebrating **Shavuot** on a kibbutz

As Jews, we're a pretty earth-conscious bunch. Think about it: Judaism pays an awful lot of attention to the *land* of Israel, its very soil and its harvests. We celebrate trees on Tu BiShevat, the wheat harvest on Shavuot, and the fruit harvest on Sukkot. There are special laws in the Torah requiring green spaces around a city and still other laws forbidding the cutting down of fruit trees. On top of all that, it's a mitzvah to care for the earth and ensure it is not ruined.

In what ways does the earth give to us?

_____

In what ways can we give back to the environment?

_____

▲ **Cleaning up** at the beach

Time to pay attention

Of course, the poor environmental conditions didn't crop up overnight. Decades of population increases and industrial growth resulted in an extreme demand on the country's natural resources. The environment suffered while attention was focused on other pressing concerns of the emerging State of Israel—absorbing large numbers of immigrants, maintaining national security, building infrastructure (basic services such as roads, schools, power lines), and developing the economy. In recent years, however, Israel has refocused its attention on the environment.

Creative solutions

Now, more than 60 years since independence, Israel's population has multiplied nearly eight-fold from eight hundred thousand to more than seven million people, industry is booming, and the country is shifting focus to the environment. Solar power is replacing imported fuel, creative solutions for providing clean water are being developed and carried out, advances in agriculture are making farming greener, air quality is on the mend thanks to clean air laws, and endangered species frolic in national parks. Israel is at the forefront of many eco-conscious technologies that serve as models for the rest of the world. Let's follow Noam, an Orthodox teenager from Tel Aviv, through a typical school day to see how environmental progress affects his life.

Solar energy

Noam's *ima* (mother) knocks firmly on his bedroom door—again—as the first rays of the morning sun peek over the horizon. Only half awake, Noam reaches for the light switch. In Noam's house, electric power comes straight from the sun. A photovoltaic system perched atop his roof converts solar energy into electricity. Because Israel has no natural fuel resources of its own, it has needed to import its energy, buying coal from countries like Australia and South Africa, and oil from countries like Mexico and Norway. Now Israel is a pioneer in solar energy, using the sun as an alternative energy source. Noam turns on the light and heads for the bathroom.

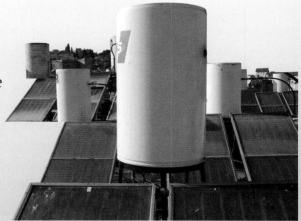

▲ **Solar water heaters** rest on rooftops all over the country. Israeli researchers continue to develop new solar technologies that turn every ray of sunshine into an invaluable natural resource without harming the environment.

solar technologies

◄ **Solar panels** on a rooftop in Tel Aviv

Desalination

Noam washes his hands in the traditional manner—pouring water three times on each hand, alternating hands. He is careful to turn off the water while brushing his teeth, he uses a water-saving toilet, and he makes sure not to dawdle in the shower. That's because water is chronically scarce in Israel, where rain generally falls only in the winter, and deserts to the south and east produce an arid climate. The water level in Lake Kinneret, which is Israel's main source of fresh water, is slowly declining, while the growing population's demand for drinking water is ever increasing.

One way that Israelis tackle the water problem is called **desalination**, removing the salt from water. Seawater and brackish water, a mixture of salt and freshwater, are plentiful in Israel, but they are too salty to drink. Israeli scientists have perfected a process called reverse osmosis that cleans salt water by filtering out salt and other chemical compounds.

▲ The government has built three **desalination plants** along the Mediterranean coast to address the country's water supply needs. The Ashkelon plant alone (pictured here) provides around 13 percent of the country's demand for tap water.

desalination plant

YOUR TURN: WATER USE

If the average bathroom faucet uses two gallons of water per minute, how much water do you use each day? Fill in your best guess for the number of minutes you run the water each day to:

brush your teeth _____   cook _____   drink _____   flush the toilet _____

wash your hands _____   water plants_____   shower _____   other _____

Total minutes: _____   Total gallons (minutes x 2): _____

Compare your results with your classmates and brainstorm ideas for using less water. How would your use of water change if you lived in Israel?

Agriculture

After reciting the morning Shaḥarit prayers, Noam is ready for breakfast. The menu this morning includes fresh-squeezed orange juice, cheese, pita, and Israeli salad. Noam washes in the prescribed manner, and says the blessing on his bread. All of the fresh produce and most of the raw ingredients that have made their way onto Noam's plate come from Israel's many farms and orchards. Although the country is small, Israel's geography provides varied climates, landscape, and soil conditions for growing a wide range of crops and raising livestock. And although the country is half desert, the determination and expertise of Israelis—from the original kibbutz farmers to the modern agrotech scientists—have turned Israel into a land flowing with milk, avocados, and Jaffa oranges.

▼ Drip irrigation

▼ An olive grove

Drip irrigation

Because water scarcity is one of Israeli agriculture's main challenges, **drip irrigation**, a technique by which precise amounts of water are delivered directly to the roots of a plant, is a common farming technique. In addition to preventing water waste, drip irrigation also protects the soil and groundwater from being contaminated by fertilizer and salt. Invented in Israel, the technique is now widely used around the globe.

Recycling water

Another way Israelis tackle the water problem is by recycling—not just paper or plastic, but human waste. Israel has emerged as a world leader in recycling sewage water and reusing it in agriculture. The Shafdan Purification Plant processes 130 million cubic meters of sewer water each year through a sophisticated purification system, resulting in water fit to irrigate the crops that will make it to Noam's breakfast table. There are no health risks, just clean, recycled water. New purification plants are under construction, and it is expected that most of the water for agriculture will eventually consist of this highly purified waste, freeing up quality fresh water for drinking and other domestic uses, like cooking and brushing teeth.

▲ A water filtration facility run by **Mekorot**, Israel's national water company

Noam finishes up his pita and Israeli salad—made from tomatoes with a 40 percent longer shelf life than most tomatoes, another Israeli achievement. He recites Birkat Hamazon (the blessing after meals) and clears the table.

BACK TO THE SOURCES

"Six years you shall sow your land and gather in its produce. And in the seventh, you shall let it rest and lie unharvested…" —Exodus 23:10-11

According to the Torah, every seven years land owned by Jewish farmers in Israel is to be left alone—no planting, no pruning, and no harvesting. The land is given a year of rest, called **sh'mitah**. Each sh'mitah year, 2,500 farmers in 100 locations across Israel observe the commandment, demonstrating their love for the land and their trust in God.

In what ways is the sh'mitah year similar to Shabbat? _____

_____

_____

Combating pollution

It's getting late, so Noam grabs his backpack full of math, science, and *halachah* (Jewish law) books and races off to catch the bus to school. Noam's bus, operated by the Egged bus company, is equipped with an environment-friendly Euro 3 engine, which uses ultra-low sulfur fuel. These buses replaced diesel buses, which—along with cars and industrial plants—were contributing to air pollution in Israel's cities. Israel's air, land, and water are all in need of a cleanup.

▼ Israel is poised to launch a revolutionary **electric car** network in 2011. These cars will run solely on electricity, with zero emissions. Battery charging stations—like gas stations, but without the gas—will be located around the country to make it easy for drivers to charge their batteries.

Air quality

In many Israeli cities, carbon monoxide and other gases produced by cars contribute to the worsening air quality. Major efforts—including a comprehensive Clean Air Law enacted in 2008—are being made to reduce vehicle emissions through legislation, supervision, and inspection. Israelis are hopeful that the plan will improve air quality and, at the same time, reduce Israel's dependence on imported oil. Noam takes a deep breath and boards the bus.

▼ Polluted water in the Jordan River

electric cars

Besides car emissions, industrial plants are some of the biggest contributors to Israel's air quality woes. In the late 1980s, a Haifa oil refinery, an electric plant, and chemical production plants spewed forth emissions that raised harmful sulfur dioxide levels in Haifa's air to more than four times the allowable level. Stricter emissions standards have since brought the pollution down to permitted levels.

Cleaning up the water

Water pollution can come from factories, from chemicals that people pour down the drain (like cleaning supplies, paints, or car oil), from overflowing sewage systems, and from pesticides and herbicides sprayed on fields and orchards.

In 1997, a bridge over the Yarkon River near Tel Aviv collapsed and members of a visiting Australian sports team fell into the water. Many of the athletes became very sick, and several even died from poisonous chemicals in the water. This tragedy was a wake-up call to many Israelis. Since then, laws have been passed to limit pollution, new sewage treatment plants have been built, and progress is being made to clean up the Yarkon River.

TURNING LANDFILLS INTO PARKS

When Ariel Sharon Park in Tel Aviv is completed in the year 2020, it will be one of the largest urban parks in the world and a symbol of renewal in Israeli environmentalism. The centerpiece of the park is the former Hiria landfill, which closed down in 1999. In 2001, the sanitation commission began the process of renewal toward a cleaner, greener future. Where once garbage trucks dumped thousands of tons of trash daily, now Noam will be able to skateboard with his friends or kick around a soccer ball in the fresh air. The 200-foot high mound provides spectacular views in all directions, as well as clean air, and park land for Tel Aviv residents.

Interview a parent or grandparent about environmental changes—for better or for worse—in your community.

Parks and wildlife

Scores of national parks and nature reserves are scattered throughout the country, and Israel works to protect the plants, animals, and other wildlife that call Israel home. The Israel Nature and Parks Authority is a government agency that reintroduces wildlife, such as gazelles, ibex, and leopards, to their natural habitats; preserves the number and variety of living things found region by region; and teaches the Israeli public about the importance of protecting nature. The Jewish National Fund, an environmental organization, has established more than 1,000 parks in Israel and planted over 240 million trees, making Israel one of only two countries in the world that actually has more trees now than it had at the beginning of the twentieth century.

▲ A young oryx

▼ The **Galilee** is a green, mountainous region in northern Israel. It includes Arab and Druze villages, Jewish and Christian holy sites, farms, nature reserves, and Lake Kinneret, Israel's primary source of fresh water.

▲ Workers in the **Hula Swamp**, circa 1940

Bringing back the swamp

The Hula Valley in northern Israel was originally swampland. In the 1950s Israel drained the swamps to turn them into farmland. Many hailed the drainage as a great achievement for Israel, but the loss of the swamps also meant the loss of a precious ecosystem, the community of fish, plants, and aquatic birds that called the swamp home.

The Hula Nature Reserve, the first nature reserve in Israel, was founded in 1964 to provide a sanctuary for tens of thousands of plants and animals. Thirty years later, Israel reflooded a part of the swamp to further revive the ecosystem. The renewed swamp also improved the quality of the water in Lake Kinneret by acting as a giant filter to prevent harmful chemical compounds from flowing southward and polluting the sea.

Hula Valley

Protecting endangered species

At another reserve, Ḥai-Bar Yotvata near Eilat in the south, endangered species that are mentioned in the Torah are nurtured and reintroduced into their natural habitats. The Arabian oryx, for example, was hunted nearly to extinction in the 1970s. Now there are over 80 oryx at Ḥai-Bar. Have you ever heard of the fennec fox? The smallest canine in the world, the fennec has huge ears that help it stay cool in the desert heat, and you can find it at Ḥai-Bar. There are now 190 nature reserves in the country, and Israeli law protects hundreds of endangered plants and animals.

▲ A fennec fox

▲ Migrating cranes take a break at the **Hula Nature Reserve**.

Ruffling a few feathers

Because Israel is at the crossroads of three continents, about 500 million birds fly over Israel twice each year while migrating between Africa, Europe, and Asia. At the same time, scores of Israeli Air Force jets fly training missions over the same limited airspace. Needless to say, when bird meets plane, it's not a pretty sight. To protect the birds—and the planes—while meeting the country's security needs, the International Center for the Study of Bird Migration in Latrun, Israel, tracks the birds. Air Force pilots avoid flying in areas that are dense with birds.

Ḥai-Bar Yotvata

DEBATE IT

In the 1950s, Israel was a young nation that depended on agriculture for economic growth. Draining the Hula Valley created much-needed farmland. But it also destroyed precious ecosystems. If you had been there, what would you have decided? Have a debate.

CREATE FARMLAND vs PROTECT THE SWAMP

What other solution can you think of?

Meeting the challenge

Israel's environmental challenges are great, but so is the Israeli commitment to dealing with them and developing solutions. Universities and other research centers focus studies on protecting water sources, controlling pollution, and restoring damaged areas. Recycling competitions, composting workshops, ads, and nature tours are teaching Israelis how to reduce, reuse, and recycle. And environmental groups throughout the country campaign for the protection, conservation, and clean-up of nature.

▲ **Recycling** is on the rise in Israel.

LIVING JEWISH VALUES: בַּל תַּשְׁחִית *Bal Tashḥit*, Do Not Destroy

Tradition tells us that God planted a magnificent garden in Eden and then brought Adam inside for the grand tour. God said, "Everything I created is for you, but make sure that you don't destroy My world. Because if you destroy it, there will be no one to fix it after you."—Ecclesiastes Rabbah 7:13

The mitzvah of *bal tashḥit*, literally "do not destroy," requires us to be careful about the way we interact with the world around us. The Earth is a precious gift and we, its caretakers, must make sure not to waste it.

With a partner, take pictures of the environment around you, and design a poster encouraging others to live according to *bal tashḥit*.

▶ Marine biologist Benjamin Kahn saw that the **coral reef** near Eilat was dying, so he and other divers collected pieces of coral that had broken off the reef and gave them to schoolchildren around the country to grow in their classrooms. Then divers carefully reattached the pieces to the reef. Today there are more than 250 species of coral and 1,200 species of fish in the beautiful coral reefs of the Red Sea.

environmental education

MEET AN ISRAELI

Sahar first became interested in ecology after she went to a workshop on making compost (natural fertilizer from kitchen and yard scraps) when she was 12 years old. Soon, she was helping to make compost for the whole kibbutz and designing a permaculture class (agriculture based on renewable natural resources) for her school.

When Sahar was 18, she decided to work with a group called Garin D'vash in Jerusalem. She helped lead workshops on living an ecologically responsible life, making recycled paper, weaving hammocks from old clothing, and making homemade soaps, creams, and toothpaste from herbs grown in community gardens.

Sahar says, "Everyone needs to know that the choices they make are important—what we eat, how we cook it, everything has an effect."

Now age 20, Sahar has been visiting and working at some of the many ecology and permaculture projects around Israel. "I don't think there is just one solution to the problems the world is facing," says Sahar. "We have to invent the lifestyle we want to live."

How is Sahar's work an expression of Jewish values and/or love of Israel? _____

_____

8 THE ECONOMY
Shekels and Cents

In the early days of the Jewish state, Israel had a more socialist economy, a system based on collective and government ownership of businesses and resources, than it does today. Many people lived in cooperative kibbutz communities, in which members contributed what they could and, in turn, received whatever they needed. In addition, the government owned banks, the telephone company, and the national airline, and health care was funded by the government for all citizens. However, Israel's economy has undergone a dramatic change since those early days.

◀ A boy herding goats on a kibbutz

Move toward capitalism

Today, only 2.5% of Israel's population lives on *kibbutzim*, and the kibbutz atmosphere has changed dramatically. Many young people prefer city life and more job options to the rural life of a kibbutz. A growing number of members work off the kibbutz, foreign workers are often hired to do the unskilled labor, and some *kibbutzim* have introduced pay scales instead of collective wages.

▲ A diverse crowd at the outdoor market in Jerusalem

▲ A Haifa **oil refinery**

As the kibbutz is changing, so is the Israeli economy. The country is moving more toward capitalism, the kind of economic system we're used to in the United States and Canada, where businesses are owned by private individuals, rather than the government. Competition encourages businesses to produce as much as possible and keep prices low. The Israeli government has privatized (transferred to private ownership) many companies it used to own, including the Bezeq phone company, the national oil company, some banks, and El Al airlines. The shift toward capitalism has dramatically changed life for many Israelis. Competition between companies has resulted in improved services, lower prices, and fewer worker strikes. Health care remains funded by the government, however, and all citizens are covered by health insurance.

YOUR TURN: ON A KIBBUTZ

Volunteering on a kibbutz has long been a tourist draw. It's fun, it's different, and it's uniquely Israeli. Tourists from around the world come to Israel to get down and dirty—they milk goats, pick avocados, or wash dishes. In the process, they also learn Hebrew, soak up some sun, and fall in love with the country.

Although agriculture remains one of Israel's primary industries, today's kibbutzim also produce metal products, electronics, chemicals, jewelry, and more.

With a parent or guardian, visit a kibbutz—online. Check out the website for a real kibbutz, and find out what industries it has. Design a poster inviting tourists to volunteer on your kibbutz.

Kibbutz

▼ **Haifa** is the third largest city in Israel and is an important port for cargo shipping and passenger traffic in the Mediterranean Sea.

▲ An airfield runway under construction

Economic need

After Israel emerged victorious from the War of Independence in 1949, the country was flat-out broke and completely overwhelmed. Israel needed to open up trade with the rest of the world, absorb tens of thousands of penniless immigrants escaping from Europe and North Africa, and build roads and hospitals—all while attempting to recover from a war that had used up almost all of its money. Israel needed a major fund-raiser.

▼ The **National Water Carrier**, a system of canals, reservoirs, pumping stations, and giant pipes, carries water from Lake Kinneret in the north to the populated center and arid south.

Israel Bonds

In 1951, the State of Israel began selling bonds to Jews living outside of Israel. A "bond" is a loan to Israel which Israel promises to repay at a later date. Israel could then use this money to build up its infrastructure. Having better roads and services in place helps businesses make money. Israel gets more money from taxes and then pays back the bonds with interest. Everybody wins: the Israeli economy gets a boost, and Jews around the world get a chance to participate in the rebuilding of the State.

▲ The only subway in Israel, the **Carmelit** was built in 1959 to connect the coastal areas of Haifa with the upper city high on Mount Carmel.

A runaway success

In 1951, the first year the program was up and running, Israel hoped to sell $25 million in bonds. It more than *doubled* that number to $52 million. Since then, Israel Bonds sales have totalled more than $26 billion. The country used some of that money to build its National Water Carrier, which makes Israel's agricultural industry possible. The money has also been used to develop Israel's ports to sell its products overseas and trade with Europe, Asia, and Africa; build alternative energy resources and power plants; improve the highway system; and build houses and create jobs for immigrants from the former Soviet Union and Ethiopia.

▲ A busy construction site

A strong economy

Today Israel enjoys a strong economy. The country is a world leader in technology and software development, and a major tourist destination. Israel has free-trade agreements, which reduce or eliminate taxes on imports and exports, with the European Union, the United States, Canada, Mexico, Jordan, and other countries. Israel ranks second among foreign countries in the number of its companies listed on the United States stock exchanges. Israel has come a long way in a very short time.

BACK TO THE SOURCES

"Without bread, there is no Torah; without Torah, there is no bread."—Pirkei Avot 3:21

This *mishnah*, or teaching, shows that we must have a strong economic base (or "bread") in order to create a strong Jewish life (or "Torah"). Or is it the other way around?

Consider the following:

In what ways might a strong or weak economy affect Jewish life?

_____

_____

How might a stronger or weaker Jewish life affect your community?

_____

_____

Wealth gaps

Despite this remarkable economic growth, the gaps between rich and poor have widened. There are more millionaires in Israel than ever, yet unemployment is high. A minimum-wage salary isn't enough to pull a family out of poverty, and cuts in social services like food subsidies and welfare have made it harder for many Israelis to make ends meet. According to a 2008 report, one out of every four Israelis lives in poverty. These are mostly the elderly, single-parent families, and large families (which are usually Arabs or ḥaredim).

Workforce

Low workforce participation also costs Israel money. Many ḥaredi men do not work but instead devote their lives to Torah study. Unemployment is high among Arabs, too. The army leads to job opportunities for many veterans, but most Arabs don't serve in the army and so

▲ A **soup kitchen** in Hebron

their job opportunities are more limited. In addition, whole industries (military industries, airports, and the water company, for example) are off-limits to Arabs for security reasons, leaving them fewer options. Many Arabs have lost their jobs as textile plants have closed and moved to cheap-labor countries like China, and jobs in agriculture have been given to foreign workers from Thailand who are willing to work for less money.

▲ Food distribution in Jerusalem

▼ A poor Arab settlement along the road to Jerusalem

Helping the needy

The Israeli government supports the unemployed and their families with welfare, health care, and other social services.

In addition, Israelis have come up with creative ways to help the needy. Volunteers from Latet distribute food to soup kitchens, welfare departments, and other nonprofit organizations. They help feed 200,000 hungry Israelis each year.

Half of all Israeli families have been helped by Yad Sarah, a charitable organization that reaches out to the elderly and disabled, and lends crutches, wheelchairs, and other medical equipment for free to anyone who needs it.

And in a popular practice called the *gemaḥ* (short for *gemilut ḥasadim*, or acts of kindness), local organizations lend money or various household items free of charge or interest. *Gemaḥ* loans might include anything from folding chairs to baby strollers to wedding dresses to Purim costumes.

▼ **Magen David Adom** is Israel's emergency aid service, responding to disasters and medical emergencies, and operating ambulances and blood banks.

MEET AN ISRAELI

Eli was born in the former Soviet Union and now lives in Tzfat. Instead of military service, he is doing national service with *Yedid*, an organization that gives free legal aid to low-income Israelis.

"The best way to help people is to empower them and give them the legal tools they need to improve their situation," Eli says.

Eli worked overtime to help a family that was about to be evicted. "The family was able to stay in their home, and they are slowly paying off their debt. I'm proud of that."

Eli plans to study social work at Tel Aviv University. "Being able to help people and your country is a wonderful feeling."

Plan a charitable organization in your home town. Think about:

Who will you help? _____

_____

How will you help them? _____

_____

What resources or people will you need to make it happen? _____

_____

What will you call your organization? _____

_____

helping the needy

Buy Israeli

Tamar is a teen who lives in Haifa. Her mother's birthday is next week, and Tamar's searching for the perfect gift. It's got to be something made in Israel, so that her money will go to Israeli businesses, which hire Israeli workers, and pay taxes to the Israeli government. Buy Israeli, her *ima* always says. So Tamar gathers the *sh'kalim* (Israeli money) she's been saving and heads to the local shopping mall.

Fashion

Tamar stops in at her *ima's* favorite clothing store. The fashion and textile (fabrics) industry is booming in Israel, with $1.1 billion worth of exports (goods sold to other countries). While some Israeli companies have their own fashion labels, more than 90 percent of Israel's exports of clothing feature familiar labels such as Donna Karan, Calvin Klein, the Gap, Banana Republic, and others. Israeli companies have also cornered the market on home textiles, including sheets, towels, and curtains. Tamar spots a handbag that would go great with one of her own outfits . . . but nothing for *ima*. She heads to the electronics store.

MADE IN ISRAEL

Flowers

The first gift idea that pops into Tamar's head is flowers. In Israel, flowers aren't just pretty, they're good business. Israel exports 1.5 billion flowers each year, and the sale of flowers and plants combined brings more than $200 million into Israel's economy.

Thanks to the country's high-tech know-how, Israel is considered a world leader in all kinds of agriculture, especially agrotechnology, which brings the world such novelties as climate-adjusted seeds and fruit-picking robots. But as much as Tamar's *ima* loves flowers, it's not quite unique enough. After all, Tamar's *abba* (father) gave her a bouquet just last week.

▲ The Israeli unit of currency is the **shekel** (plural: *sh'kalim*).

PIONEERING SPIRIT

Lea Gottlieb and her husband Armin had owned a raincoat factory in Budapest. But in 1949, they made aliyah to Israel, where rain is so scarce that we pray for it. They needed a new idea, so they turned to swimsuits.

With a good idea and a pioneering spirit, Leah set to work. She sold her wedding ring to buy fabric, borrowed a sewing machine, and founded Gottex, which today is an internationally known swimsuit manufacturer. The original designs were inspired by the vivid colors of Israel—the aqua of the Mediterranean Sea, the golden yellow of the desert, the pink of Jerusalem stone, and the greens of the Galilee.

What other products might the varied landscapes of Israel inspire?

_____

_____

_____

_____

OUTDOOR MARKETS

You name it, Maḥane Yehuda has probably got it. The open air *shuk* in Jerusalem contains hundreds of stalls and shops that sell everything from vegetables, raw meat, baked goods, and spices, to household appliances, jewelry, and Judaica. Each stall specializes in something.

Shopping in the *shuk* is an experience filled with brilliant colors, smells, and noise. Street musicians perform for passersby while vendors yell out prices. The unique atmosphere, sheer quantity of merchandise, and reasonable prices attract Jewish, Arab, and tourist shoppers alike.

Other famous Israeli markets include Shuk Hacarmel in Tel Aviv and the *shuk* in the Arab Quarter of the Old City of Jerusalem.

With a friend, plan your own model Israeli *shuk*. What will you sell?

shuk

▲ Hebrew University of Jerusalem

Research and development

There are some good gift options in the electronics store, but they're way out of Tamar's price range. Research and development for Israeli inventions, from communications equipment to agricultural innovations to military advances, takes place in universities, public research institutes, medical centers, and government research centers.

With the world's highest percentage of engineers relative to the general population, many of whom immigrated to Israel in the late 1980s from the former Soviet Union, Israel has the engineering brainpower it needs to get the job done. Drawing on this wealth of talent, American technology companies like Motorola, Yahoo, Microsoft, Google, IBM, and Intel have established research centers in Israel where they develop new technologies they can sell around the globe.

▶ The Google building in Haifa

innovations

Medical advances

Israelis have also made major contributions to health care and advanced medical technology. For example, an Israeli company invented a tiny camera that patients can swallow like a pill so doctors can examine their insides easily and painlessly. Israeli researchers have developed medicines to slow the advance of multiple sclerosis and a device synchronized with the heart that helps patients with heart failure. In addition, Israeli company Teva Pharmaceutical is the world's largest manufacturer of generic drugs. Israel is a clear world leader in technology, and money is pouring into Israel from foreign investors to help develop more.

COOL INVENTIONS

These Israeli innovations are just the tip of the iceberg. What will they think of next?

▶ **Cell Phones:** The cell phone was invented in Israel by Motorola, and most of the latest technology inside it was also invented by Israeli engineers.

▲ **Jellyfish Repellent:** Jellyfish stings can spoil any day at the beach. But an Israeli company has invented an anti-jellyfish sting lotion.

▼ **Instant Messenger:** Four Israelis developed ICQ, the original instant messenger technology. They came up with the idea during a ping pong game in Herzliya in 1996, then sold it to America Online in 1998 for $407 million.

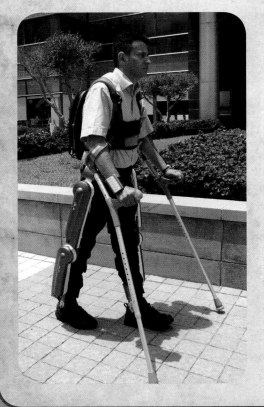

◀ **Robotic Skeleton:** A company based in Haifa has invented a robotic exoskeleton, a device that enables paralyzed people to stand, walk, or even climb stairs. Good-bye wheelchair!

Tourism

Tamar has another great idea for her mother's birthday gift—a guided tour. From hiking in the Golan Heights, to climbing Masada, praying at the Western Wall, floating in the Dead Sea, visiting the Megiddo archaeological site, and snorkeling in Eilat, travelers from around the world are attracted to Israel's unique combination of history, culture, religion, and nature.

▲ Looking out over the ramparts of the Old City of Jerusalem

▲ Floating in the Dead Sea

In 2009, more than 2.7 million people visited Israel, contributing $3.3 billion to the economy, and supporting 88,800 jobs. The largest number of tourists comes from the United States. Visitors include Jews coming to celebrate holidays (especially Sukkot and Passover), Christians coming on religious pilgrimages, and teens touring the country.

▼ Enjoying the beach in Eilat

▲ Visiting a camel ranch

The health of the tourism industry fluctuates with perceptions of Israeli security. Tourists are often scared by news reports of threats to Israel, but visiting Israel is actually very safe. Even including terrorism, there are fewer homicides in Israel than in major North American cities. Tamar decides she'll take her mother for a guided tour of Ein Gedi, with its waterfalls and caves not far from the Dead Sea. After a vigorous hike and a dip in the natural pools, they'll tour some of the ancient synagogue ruins. They'll play tourists for the day and support Israel's economy at the same time.

▲ Exploring waterfalls and caves at Ein Gedi

tourism

▲ Reciting **Shaḥarit** (morning prayers) at Masada

▼ Tourists working on a kibbutz

9 CONNECTING WITH ISRAEL

Justin's back home, adjusting to the ten-hour time difference between Israel and Seattle. It was an eye-opening trip and one of those times in his life that Justin hopes he never forgets. He visited some awesome places, picked up a major taste for shawarma (how did he ever live without it?!), and kept some shekel coins as souvenirs. Now he's at the computer, uploading his pictures and making a memory book on his favorite photo website. Let's peek over his shoulder as he remembers some of his favorite adventures.

"Israel is such an interesting mix of contrasts—where else would you see a camel in the middle of a big, bustling city? The variety of different cultures, and the mix of new and old, sometimes come together in startling ways."

"We learned about Israel's government on a tour of the Knesset in Jerusalem. Israel is a democratic country, and at the same time it's a Jewish country. This leads to some interesting debates, such as whether buses should run on Shabbat. We had some good times debating politics with every single cab driver we met. It seems everyone in Israel has an opinion about everything, and they're not shy about sharing it."

"This is a military jeep near the Arab city of Hebron, in the West Bank. Although security is a major challenge for Israel— and I mean major, as in bomb shelters, checkpoints, and guards at entrances to banks and stores—I always felt safe when I was there."

"I bought souvenirs at a shuk—IDF T-shirts for my friends, Naot sandals for my mom, an olive-wood tzedakah box for my dad, and a colorful scarf for my sister. It felt good to help out Israel's economy by buying things made in Israel."

"I've never seen people from so many different cultures in one place before. The different groups don't always understand each other, but they're working on overcoming tensions. I listened to a band made up of Jewish and Bedouin musicians."

"This is a picture of camels that I saw at Ein Gedi, an amazing nature reserve with caves, springs, a waterfall, and all kinds of animals and plants I've never seen before. That day we also climbed Masada, the site of an ancient fortress, and swam in the salty waters of the Dead Sea. The parks and nature reserves in Israel are amazing, and there are so many of them packed into such a small country."

"The Kinneret, the lake in this picture, is Israel's main source of fresh water, but its water level is getting lower and lower. Israelis are coming up with all kinds of cool ideas to help solve the water-shortage problem, like filtering out salt from seawater and recycling sewage water. I had to be careful about conserving water and taking shorter showers because water is so precious."

"I got to try my hand at being an archaeologist at a dig in Tiberias. I had a blast digging and sifting through the ruins of an ancient town. A guy in my group found a really cool oil lamp. He actually held in his hand something that hadn't been touched in more than two thousand years!"

"Yad Vashem is Israel's national Holocaust memorial, commemorating the six million Jews and the many communities that were wiped out in the Holocaust. They also have a walkway called Avenue of the Righteous among the Nations, dedicated to non-Jews who risked their lives to save Jews. I noticed one plaque with the name Oskar Schindler, which I recognized from the movie Schindler's List."

"Judaism is everywhere in this country. I saw secular, religious, and ultra-Orthodox Jews from a wide variety of backgrounds, including someone having a bar mitzvah at the Kotel."

"We went to a Hapoel soccer game. Those guys are awesome. We've also been to all sorts of other cool places, like the Jerusalem Biblical Zoo, a kosher McDonald's (yup, only in Israel!), and even a concert in an ancient amphitheater. What was I worried about? There's plenty of stuff to do, see, and experience in this tiny country. And I found a basketball game almost every day."

"All the street signs and many other signs, too, are in Hebrew, Arabic, and English. My Hebrew improved a lot while I was in Israel. Whenever I asked for directions or ordered food in a restaurant I tried my best to do it in Hebrew."

Imagine yourself in Israel. Attach your own photo or drawing, and write a caption describing what you might see or do there.

_____

_____

_____

_____

_____

_____

PLAN A VISIT

Now imagine you're planning a ten-day visit to Israel. What would you like to see and do there? Will you go snorkeling in Eilat? Buy souvenirs at the shuk in Tel Aviv? Visit an art gallery in Tzfat? Make a list and mark them on the map. The Kotel has already been marked as an example. Share your completed map with your classmates.

Day 1: _Visit the Kotel_

Day 2: _____

Day 3: _____

Day 4: _____

Day 5: _____

Day 6: _____

Day 7: _____

Day 8: _____

Day 9: _____

Day 10: _____

Back home in America, there's plenty you can do to connect with Israel from afar. You might find an Israeli pen pal, buy Israeli products, or learn more about Israel so you can represent Israel's side in a debate with your friends. How else can you nurture a connection with Israel?

Kotel, in Jerusalem

Israel in maps

N
W   E
S

0   50 MI

0   50 KM

SAY IT IN HEBREW

Are you ready to brush up on your Hebrew? Try out these words and phrases.

Basics

שָׁלוֹם	Hello/good-bye/peace
כֵּן	Yes
לֹא	No
לְהִתְרָאוֹת!	See you later
תּוֹדָה רַבָּה	Thank you
בְּבַקָּשָׁה	Please/you're welcome
סְלִיחָה	Excuse me
אֶתְמוֹל	Yesterday
הַיּוֹם	Today
מָחָר	Tomorrow
אֲרוּחַת בֹּקֶר	Breakfast
אֲרוּחַת צָהֳרַיִם	Lunch
אֲרוּחַת עֶרֶב	Dinner
אוֹטוֹבּוּס	Bus
רַכֶּבֶת	Train
מוֹנִית	Taxi
רְחוֹב	Street
יָמִין	Right (direction)
שְׂמֹאל	Left
יָשָׁר	Straight ahead

Questions and Phrases

מִי?	Who…?
מַה?	What…?
אֵיפֹה?	Where…?
מָתַי?	When…?
לָמָּה?	Why…?
כַּמָּה . . . ?	How much/many…?
כַּמָּה זֶה עוֹלֶה?	How much does this cost?
אַתָּה מְדַבֵּר אַנְגְּלִית? \ אַתְּ מְדַבֶּרֶת אַנְגְּלִית?	Do you speak English? (to m/f)
מַה נִשְׁמַע?	How are you (what's going on)?
מַה שְׁלוֹמְךָ?\ מַה שְׁלוֹמֵךְ?	How are you (well-being)? (to m/f)
אֲנִי לֹא מֵבִין.\ אֲנִי לֹא מְבִינָה.	I don't understand. (m/f)
מַה שִׁמְךָ? \ מַה שְׁמֵךְ?	What's your name? (to m/f)
שְׁמִי . . .	My name is….
אֲנִי רוֹצֶה \ אֲנִי רוֹצָה . . .	I would like…. (m/f)
מַה הַשָּׁעָה?	What time is it?
אֵיפֹה הַשֵּׁירוּתִים?	Where is the bathroom?

Days of the Week

יוֹם רִאשׁוֹן	Sunday
יוֹם שֵׁנִי	Monday
יוֹם שְׁלִישִׁי	Tuesday
יוֹם רְבִיעִי	Wednesday
יוֹם חֲמִישִׁי	Thursday
יוֹם שִׁשִׁי	Friday
שַׁבָּת	Saturday/Shabbat

Numbers

אֶפֶס	0
אַחַת	1
שְׁתַּיִם	2
שָׁלֹשׁ	3
אַרְבַּע	4
חָמֵשׁ	5
שֵׁשׁ	6
שֶׁבַע	7
שְׁמֹנֶה	8
תֵּשַׁע	9
עֶשֶׂר	10

▼ Dramatic mountains in the Negev Desert

RESOURCES

How will you experience Israel? Check out these resources and make a connection to our homeland.

EXPLORE

• Use **Modern Israel Online** to explore modern Israel through games, videos, photos, art, music, activities, and more. www.behrmanhouse.com/EMI

• **BabagaNewz** is a fun and educational website for Jewish middle-school students and teachers to explore Jewish values, traditions, life-cycle events, holidays, and Israel. www.babaganewz.com/tags/israel

• Visit the **Behrman House** website for Hebrew games and resources. www.behrmanhouse.com

• Check out **Eye on Israel**, an interactive map of Israel, with information on many sites in Israel. www.eyeonisrael.com

• The **Israel Ministry of Tourism** has a tourist website full of eye-catching photos and interesting facts about places in Israel. www.goisrael.com

VISIT

• **Taglit-Birthright Israel** provides free educational trips to Israel for Jewish young adults ages 18 to 26. www.birthrightisrael.com

• Other **teen programs** to Israel are sponsored by the North American Federation of Temple Youth (NFTY), United Synagogue Youth (USY), Camp Ramah, Young Judea, BBYO, Friends of Israel Scouts, and other organizations.

CONNECT

• **Epals** can connect your class to classrooms in Israel. www.epals.com

• **Jewish National Fund** connects Jews around the world with Israel through environmental projects. www.jnf.org

READ

• *D"ash* is the Israeli magazine for English-speaking young people around the world. Read about fashion, food, music, and sports, and meet young Israelis in high school and in the army. www.jpost.com

• Visit **My Jewish Learning** to find interesting information about Israel—and all things Jewish. www.myjewishlearning.com

• **Jewish Virtual Library** is a comprehensive online Jewish encyclopedia. www.jewishvirtuallibrary.org

▼ Ein Gedi, an oasis in the desert

GLOSSARY

A

Aliyah: literally "going up," *making aliyah* means immigrating to Israel. An aliyah during a prayer service is the honor of being called up to the Torah to recite the blessing.

Ashkenazic: a Jew of German or European descent.

B

Baha'i: a faith founded in nineteenth-century Persia that emphasizes the spiritual unity of humankind.

Balfour Declaration: a British policy statement issued in 1917 that promised support for a Jewish homeland.

Bedouin: nomadic or semi-nomadic Arabs who live primarily in desert areas; many have settled in villages and are no longer nomadic.

Beta Israel: Ethiopian Jews said to be descended from King Solomon.

C

Chief Rabbinate: the recognized religious authority of the Jewish people in Israel, which oversees many aspects of religious life, including *kashrut*, marriage, and divorce.

D

Dabke: a popular Arab folk dance.

Desalination: the process of removing salt from seawater, in order to provide fresh water for drinking, washing, agriculture, or other uses.

Diaspora: the many places outside the Land of Israel where Jews live, having dispersed after the Romans destroyed the Second Temple in 70 CE and exiled the community.

Disengagement Plan: Israeli Prime Minister Ariel Sharon's plan that evicted Israeli settlers from the Gaza Strip and four settlements in the West Bank in 2005.

Dreyfus Affair: a flagrant act of anti-Semitism in 1895 that falsely accused Captain Alfred Dreyfus, a French Jew, of spying, and inspired the Zionist movement.

Drip irrigation: a highly-efficient farming technique that delivers small amounts of water directly to the roots of a plant.

Druze: an Arabic-speaking religious community that represents less than 2 percent of Israel's population.

E

Eid al Fitr: a Muslim holiday that marks the end of fasting during the month of Ramadan.

F

Falafel: fried balls of ground chickpeas served in a pita filled with sauces, salads, and pickles.

First Aliyah: a wave of mass immigration to Israel (1882-1902) of some 35,000 people mostly from Eastern Europe.

First Temple: known as Solomon's Temple, it stood on the site that is now the Temple Mount in Jerusalem for hundreds of years, until it was destroyed by Babylonian King Nebuchadnezzar II in 586 BCE.

G

Gaza Strip or **Gaza:** a small strip of land on the Mediterranean Sea bordering Egypt and Israel that was captured by Israel in 1967 during the Six-Day War. Palestinian-populated areas have been under Palestinian self-rule since 1994.

Gemah: short for *gemilut ḥasadim*, or acts of kindness, a popular practice in which local organizations lend money or household items free of charge to those in need.

H

Halachah: Jewish religious law from the Torah and Talmud.

Hamas: a fundamentalist Islamic group that won Palestinian elections in Gaza in 2006 and is committed to destroying Israel.

Ḥaredi: an ultra-orthodox Jew (plural: *ḥaredim*).

"Hatikvah": literally "hope," Israel's national anthem, which was originally a Zionist hymn.

Hezbollah: a radical Muslim terrorist group in Lebanon committed to the destruction of Israel.

I

Intifada: "shaking off" in Arabic, a violent uprising by Palestinians in the disputed territories of Gaza and the West Bank, from 1987-1993.

Israel Defense Forces or **IDF:** Israel's military forces, including army, navy, and air force. The IDF is commonly known in Israel by the Hebrew acronym *Tzahal*.

K

Kashrut: Jewish dietary laws prohibiting certain foods, and requiring that milk and meat be kept separate and that kosher animals be slaughtered in a specific way.

Kibbutz: a community in which land and property is communally owned, and responsibilities for child-care and other social services are shared (plural: *kibbutzim*).

Klezmer: Jewish folk music that originated among Ashkenazic Jews of Eastern Europe.

Knesset: Israel's parliament, responsible for making the country's laws.

Kotel, or **Western Wall:** in Jerusalem, the remains of the Second Temple's western retaining wall; Judaism's most sacred place for pilgrimage and prayer.

L

Law of Return: an Israeli law that grants Jews from anywhere in the world the right to return to Israel and become Israeli citizens.

M

Maccabiah Games: an international competition often called the "Jewish Olympics." The games take place in Israel and are open to Jewish athletes from around the world, and to all Israeli citizens regardless of religion or ethnicity.

Masorti Movement: a traditional, egalitarian religious movement in Israel, affiliated with the worldwide Conservative movement.

Mizrahi: a Jew of Middle Eastern or North African descent (plural: *Mizrahim*).

Mosque: a place of worship for followers of Islam.

Muslim: literally "one who submits" in Arabic; a follower of Islam, one of the major religions of the world which teaches that there is only one God and Muhammad is God's prophet.

N

Nakba: literally "catastrophe" in Arabic; the Palestinian name for Israel's War of Independence in 1948.

National Service or **Sherut Leumi:** an alternative voluntary service for those who cannot or do not wish to serve in the Israel Defense Forces.

O

Olim: immigrants to Israel.

P

Palestine: the name of the land where the modern State of Israel is located from ancient times until the founding of the state in 1948; the term is also used for a future independent state for the Palestinian people.

Palestine Liberation Organization or **PLO:** an organization that represents the Palestinian people in all military, political, and financial endeavors.

Parliamentary democracy: a multiparty system of government in which the party that wins the most seats during an election forms the government.

Partition Plan: a United Nations plan to separate Palestine into Jewish and Arab states. The UN General Assembly approved this plan in November 1947, leading to the establishment of the State of Israel.

Pogroms: organized massacres and riots against Jews in Eastern Europe.

Progressive Judaism: a liberal religious movement in Israel, affiliated with the worldwide Progressive movement, which includes the Reform and Reconstructionist movements.

R

Ramadan: the ninth month of the Islamic calendar during which Muslims fast to learn patience, humility, and spirituality.

Refuseniks: Jews of the former Soviet Union who had been denied permission to immigrate to other countries.

S

Sabra: a Jew born in Israel.

Second Aliyah: a wave of mass immigration to Israel (1904-1914) of 40,000 Jews, who were escaping increasing levels of anti-Semitism in Russia.

Second Intifada: a violent Palestinian uprising that began in 2000 and targeted Israeli soldiers and civilians with violent attacks and suicide bombings.

Second Temple: in Jerusalem, the center of Jewish life between 516 BCE and 70 CE, when it was destroyed by the Romans.

Secular: not pertaining to or connected with religion.

Security fence: a barrier separating Israel proper from the West Bank, begun during the Second Intifada to protect Israel from Palestinian terrorist attacks.

Sephardic: a Jew of Spanish or Portuguese descent.

Shekel: a unit of Israel's currency (plural: *sh'kalim*).

Sh'mitah: literally "release," the seventh year of a seven-year agricultural cycle in which land is allowed to rest without any planting.

Shuk: an open-air market.

Sigd: an Israeli national holiday, celebrated by Ethiopian Jews, commemorating acceptance of the Torah at Mount Sinai.

Six-Day War: the war fought in 1967 between Egypt, Jordan, and Syria against Israel, instigated by Egypt's blockade of the Straits of Tiran.

Socialist economy: an economy based on public or common ownership of all resources.

T

Tzofim: the Israel Scouts Federation, Israel's national scouting club.

U

Ulpan: an intensive Hebrew-language class.

W

War of Independence: the war fought in 1948 and 1949 between the newly created State of Israel and neighboring Arab countries.

West Bank: the area between the Jordan River and the 1949 final demarcation line between Israel and Jordan that was seized by Israel in 1967 during the Six-Day War. In 1993, Palestinian population centers in this disputed territory were transferred to the Palestinian Authority.

The White City: a neighborhood of Tel Aviv with more than 4,000 structures built in the 1930s by immigrant German Jewish architects in the Bauhaus style of simple, asymmetrical shapes.

White Paper: a 1939 document issued by the British government that declared their intent for Palestine to become an independent state and restricted Jewish immigration to ensure an Arab majority there.

Y

Yeshiva: an institute of learning where students study sacred Hebrew texts such as the Torah and Talmud.

Yom Ha'atzma'ut: Israel Independence Day, celebrated on the fifth day of Iyar, corresponding to April or May on the Gregorian calendar.

Yom Hazikaron: Israeli Fallen Soldiers and Victims of Terrorism Remembrance Day.

Yom Kippur War: an attack on Israel by Egypt and Syria, on Yom Kippur in 1973, ending with a cease-fire one month later.

Yom Yerushalayim: Jerusalem Day, a national holiday commemorating the reunification of Jerusalem during the Six-Day War.

Z

Zionism: the movement to establish and support a Jewish state in the Land of Israel.

INDEX

The publisher gratefully acknowledges the following sources of photographs and graphic images:
(B=bottom, C=center, L=left, R=right, T=top)

American Jewish Archives: 56 (B); Rami Aolyan: 69 (TR); Risa Towbin Aqua: 11 (C); Argo Medical Technologies Ltd: 97 (BL); Art Resource, NY: Bildarchiv Preussischer Kulturbesitz 52 (TL), Jewish Chronicle Archive/HIP 52 (TR), The Jewish Museum of New York 50 (T), Visual Arts Library 18 (L); Kim Beame: 44 (C), 95 (CR); Karin Beitel: 21 (TR), 29 (C), 35 (CR); David Behrman: 86 (T); Behrman House: 33 (B); Bigstock: Noam Armonn 29 (TR), Diana Amster 34 (CR), Ryan Rodrick Beiler 66 (TR), 67 (B), Dusty Cline 22 (TR), Nadejda Degtyareva 10 (CL), Steven Frame 49 (CL), Joshua Haviv 48-49 (B), Alexander Klampert 73 (TL), Herbert Kratky 104 (T), Georgy Markov 20 (TR), Abba Richman 91 (BR), David Snyder 68 (TL, CL), Harry Tucker 67 (TL), Lisa Young 91 (BL); Blue Flower Arts: 17 (BR); Ortal Buchbut: 47 (T); Hannah Christenson: 28 (BR); Dreamstime: Sergey Aleksandrov 92 (B), Noam Armonn 80-81 (B), 89 (TL), Pavel Bernshtam 85 (C), Yehuda Bernstein 19 (TR), Bonfils Fabien 82 (C), Dr. N. Gidal 50 (CR), Vincent Giordano 20 (C), Gkuna 10-11 (B), Greeneinav 22 (CL), Yana Gulyanovska 79 (C), Jfragments 34 (T), Karin Hildebrand Lau 36 (TR), Chris Lockey 81 (B), Mazor 57 (C), Noamfein 46-47 (B), Thomas Schmitt 70 (TL), Yoavsinai 66 (B), Roman Zaremba 50 (BL); Vered Feinberg and Noa Lencovsky: 11 (T); Friends of the Israel Scouts, Inc.: 23 (T); Elisha Frumkin: 9 (drummer); Getty Images: David Buimovitch 79 (T), Khaled Desouki 92 (T), Menahem Kahana 32 (B), Stephen Jaffe 74 (T), Beshara Louai 25 (C), Oleg Nikishin 25 (T), 37 (Awad), David Silverman 39; Gila Gevirtz: 27 (C), 45 (C), 46 (C), 70 (TL), 90 (C), 93 (B); Bartzi Goldblat: 37 (Casay, Kahalani); Tammy Gottlieb for the Masorti movement: 43 (T); Sahar Hofi: 87 (T); Israel Defense Forces: 73 (R); Israel Ministry of Tourism: 8 (T, B), 9 (TL, TC, TR, tent), 14, 15 (B), 19 (B), 21 (B), 22 (CR), 22-23 (B), 24-25 (B), 30 (BL), 35 (BL), 38 (B), 44 (TL), 89 (TR), 96 (T), 98 (TR), 98-99 (B), 99 (TL, TR), 101 (TL, B), 102, 103; Israelimages: Israel Talby 78 (C), 83 (T); iStockphoto: NirAlon 33 (T), Robert Harris (Torah icon, multiple pages), Peter Zelei (parchment background, multiple pages); Terry Kaye: 15 (TR), 34 (B), 64 (T), 77 (TR); Nir Kedar/Peres Center for Peace 75 (T); Mordechai Meiri: 40-41 (B); Naamani: 40 (TL); National Photo Collection: Einat Anker 36 (B), Fritz Cohen 59 (T), David Eldan 54 (T), Amos Ben Gershom 16 (TR), 23 (B), 37 (BL), 60, Zoltan Kluger 17 (TL, BL), 52 (B), 55, 58, 58-59 (B), 84 (TR), 90 (T), Tsvika Israeli 31 (C), 32 (T, C), 54 (C), Moshe Milner 13, 15 (TL), 35 (T), 46 (TL), 61 (TL), 65 (R), 69 (TL), 81 (T), Mark Neyman 29 (B), 57 (R), Avi Ohayon 17 (TR), 24 (T), 44-45 (B), 62 (B), 70 (TR), 90 (B), Hans Pinn 30 (BR), 56 (T), 57 (B), Ze'ev Spector 61 (TR), Sa'ar Ya'acov 19 (TL), 41 (T, C), 61 (C), 62 (TR), 74 (T, B), Ofer Yizhar 72 (TL), Unknown 53 (T); Andrew Neusner: 63; New Line Productions, Inc.: 26 (T); Otzarstock: Ezra Landau 26 (BL), 82 (T), 92 (C); Peace Child Israel: 75 (L); Richard Nowitz Photography: 29 (TL), 30 (BL), 42 (R), 46 (B), 49 (TR), 77 (TL), 80 (T, C), 99 (B); Howard Rosenbaum: 28 (T), 72-73 (B); Samuel A. Cohen/Adiv Photography: 84 (TL), 86 (B), 88 (TL), 99 (CL); Seeds of Peace: 75 (B); Shutterstock: Andresr 97 (BR), Ariy 12 (T) , Arkady 28 (BL), B & T Media Group Inc. 71 (CR), Jill Battaglia 20(BL), Ryan Rodrick Beiler 71 (T), Pavel Bernshtam 67 (CR), 68-69 (B), Bomshtein 2-3, Ronen Boidek 64 (B), Yehuda Boltshauser 70-71 (B), Brian Chase (cover teens), Lars Christensen (cover sky), Nir Darom 8 (C), Boris Diakovsky 50-51 (B), 51 (TL), Dejan Gileski 10-11 (B), 40 (TR), Gorshkov25 (cover Kotel), Alex Gul 76-77 (B), Ido 42-43 (B), Ifong 71 (CL), Alexander Ishchenko 9 (pillars), Elena Itsenko 21 (TL), k45025 107, Kavram 1, 106, 112, Stephan Kerkhofs 97 (T), Kiselilimun 95 (TR), John Kropewnicki 88 (TR), Keith Levit 38 (T), Mikhail Levit 18 (cup), 37 (T), 40, 45 (TR), 65 (B), 100, David Mckee 67 (TR), 104 (C), Eoghan McNally 22 (TL), Christine B. Miller 76 (TR), Mishella 49 (CR), mmattner (cover camel), Christian Musat 85 (TR), Irina Opachevsky 94-95 (B), PardoY 9 (ibex), Christopher Parypa 10 (T), Dmitry Pistrov (cover Tel Aviv night), Pmphone 97 (TR), Dmitry Popov 31 (T), Lev Radin 95 (T), S1001 94 (C), Elisei Shafer 87 (B), Slavapolo 6-7 (B), 84-85 (B), 91 (TR), Jason Stitt 16 (T), Albert H. Teich 9 (shrine), Robert Paul Van Beets 98 (TL), Vblinov 4-5, VojtechVlk 36 (TL), WitR 82-83 (B); Abir Sultan: 27 (B); Sasson Tiram/ Jewish Agency for Israel: 33 (C); Eli Vidal: 93 (T); Cheryl Vogel: 20 (BR); Michael Weinberg: 96 (B); Aviva Werner: 18 (B), 78 (B); Yutacan/Wikipedia Commons: 88-89 (B).

▼ Picturesque mountains near the Dead Sea

EXPERIENCE
Modern
ISRAEL

Aviva Werner

Behrman House Publishers

www.behrmanhouse.com
www.behrmanhouse.com/EMI

EXPERIENCE
Modern
ISRAEL